Rosemaris Campos
WM 2007

Confessions
of a Christian Wife

A Look at *Relationships* and *Faith*

Also by Heather Thompson Day

Cracked Glasses

The God Myth and Other Lies

Hook, Line, and Sinker

How to Feed the Mediavore

Life After Eden

Confessions
of a Christian Wife

A Look at *Relationships* and *Faith*

DR. HEATHER THOMPSON DAY

Pacific Press®
Publishing Association
Nampa, Idaho | www.pacificpress.com

Cover design by Gerald Lee Monks
Cover design resources from iStockphoto.com | Inquieta
Inside design by Aaron Troia

The author assumes full responsibility for the accuracy of all facts and quotations as cited in this book.

Additional copies of this book may be purchased by calling toll-free 1-800-765-6955 or by visiting AdventistBookCenter.com.

ISBN 978-0-8163-6464-0

November 2018

Contents

Confessions of a Christian Wife

I think people would be happier if they admitted things more often. In a sense we are all prisoners of some memory, or fear, or disappointment—we are all defined by something we can't change.
—Simon Van Booy

I am just going to come right out and say it—Christians can be fake. If I have just caused you to squint your eyes, then first, you need to understand that I am one of you. I'm not just an Easter and Christmas Christian. I'm not the Christian who only thinks Scripture is good for Instagram selfies. I'm hard core. I've read the Bible cover to cover more times than I've binged *Back to the Future*, and trust me, that's a lot. I attended church school for the majority of my education, and I play Bible trivia games for fun. I can answer which servant of Saul introduced David to Mephibosheth without using Google. (Ziba. Thanks for playing.)

This isn't a criticism of the church from the outside; this is coming from someone who can turn to a song in the hymnal faster than you can locate it on Pandora. I feel more romantic about Christ each day I'm alive, and so I hope we can be adults here and have a real conversation. Oftentimes, Christians are fake, and it's a turnoff.

When I first decided I was really going to do this religion thing, I, too, thought this meant I had to be perfect. Timehop graciously shows me my old status updates, and I legit want to throw up in my mouth each time. I was like a sugar-coated peep dipped in caramel and then slathered in chocolate icing: too sweet. No one's buying that.

I didn't want anyone to question whether I had a sincere relationship with God, so I tried to say the right thing at all times and even felt a need to prove that I was a good person. Somewhere along the way, I think God was like, "K, girl, chill out," and I went through the strangely difficult process of allowing myself to be who I actually am. I tried to be the perfect Christian, and it turns out that God just needed me to be myself.

I know I'm not alone in this because hello newsfeed! I see it all the time. Christians trying to outdo one another in their Christianness. Everyone pretending they have it all together. Making sure that every good deed doesn't go without a notification and photo op. But look fam, that's not who Christ was.

The Bible says to give in such a way that your left hand doesn't know what your right hand has done. (See Matthew 6:3.) Christ didn't wait till there was a crowd to begin His sermon. He would get so lost in a compelling conversation with one person that others gathered. I had a professor who told me once that no one is ever converted from the pulpit. If you want to make an impact, you have to get off the stage and start having some real conversations with some real people as the real you. You don't have to post photos of your Bible or Hebrew tattoo to prove that you like Jesus. Just be kind and respectful. Give to people who need help. Spend your energy trying to boost others, rather than looking for ways for others to boost you. Live in such a humble, gracious, loving way that people just want to be next to you—all different types of people. Not just other Christian people. Because PS, that's how Christianity works.

Whenever we try too hard to convince others of something, I worry that we're actually trying to convince ourselves. I have spent the last couple of years focusing on showing God, rather than other people, who I am. I'd say that it was easy, but it wasn't. My natural instinct is to love the crowd, the compliments, and the attention. But if you read through the Gospels, you will find very quickly that Christ actually let Himself get lost in a crowd, wasn't looking for compliments, and never sought out attention. The Man was the embodiment of humility, and if anyone should have acted like He walked on water, uh, well—Christ!

So stop faking it. Stop with the awkward sermonizing of pain. Stop smiling to people's faces if you are going to whisper behind their backs. Stop pretending that your kids are perfect. OK, so I totally do that, but only because they are under seven. How bad can they be? It's too soon for me to worry about running random drug tests. Right now, my biggest concern is getting them to stop leaving poop stains in their underpants. #THESTRUGGLEISREAL.

Stop pretending like your marriage is perfect. Don't get me wrong, I'm *obsessed* with my husband. But I'd be lying if I didn't admit that I've stood in the driveway, screaming at his taillights once—or ten times—in our marriage. My apologies to our neighbors.

Stop the holier-than-thou spiel. Stop the hypocrisy. Stop quoting 1 Corinthians 13 and then laughing at racist jokes. Stop pretending as if you've never stubbed your toe and dropped an expletive (*shut up*, we are all sinners).

Christianity is about coming to God as you are, and hoping that each day He will help you put a little more good into a world with a lot of bad juju. It's about genuinely loving God and genuinely loving people. The world doesn't need more perfect Christians. But it does need more authentic ones.

For the next thirty-one days, I am going to be real with you. We are going to talk strategies for love and pain. We will go through relationship do's and don'ts. We will discuss what happens in marriage and how I'm still trying to be a real Christian. I am going to be honest about what I have found that works in my life and marriage and what doesn't. This book isn't about filters or Photoshop. I made a pact with God when I was twenty-two years old that if He ever allowed me to publish a book, I would be honest about who I was. So this is me being honest about the fact that sometimes I fail as a Christian, a wife, and a mother. But I can also tell you that I genuinely love God and I genuinely love people. That seems like a good place to start.

So here is to thirty-one days of being real and being a better wife.

Bible Verse for Reflection

"Therefore each of you must put off falsehood and speak truthfully to your neighbor, for we are all members of one body" (Ephesians 4:25).

Questions

Ask your partner to go through these questions with you each day for the next thirty-one days. You will need to work together.

- What would you like to be more honest with yourself about?
- What do you hope to improve about your marriage in the next thirty-one days?

The Lucifer Effect

The world is not fair, and often fools, cowards,
liars and the selfish hide in high places.
—Bryant H. McGill

I am your token millennial. I was born in 1987. (You can check my driver's license should you feel skeptical.) I am young enough to use Google as a verb but old enough to have owned mixtapes. I refuse to shop at Walmart because of the labor conditions in their Asian factories, and yet I will admit I have no idea who my state representatives are.

That is the millennial generation. A passionate sea of contradiction and controversy. Our parents told us that we could follow our dreams and our hearts. As a result, we travel on a dime and fight for the acceptance of all people, while at the same time being the most narcissistic generation in history by a long shot. It's almost as if millennials are pinned between technology and a deep need for fulfillment, so we grab onto the new, while feeling nostalgia for the way things used to be.

Millennials are many things; one of which is depressed. We are constantly connected, and yet studies show that when asked how many trusted confidants millennials have outside of their families, the most common answer is *zero*. Basically, those twelve-hundred-plus friends on your social media wouldn't even let you watch their cat.

We are the generation of hashtags and filters. Everything is created to project an image of who we want to be, which is never what we actually are. We try our hardest to be witty in 140 characters or less. We post

11

photos of our night out, and the scene is always much more intriguing than the night actually was. I think some of this is the reason we often feel unfulfilled. We want everyone around us to think we have it all together—but we don't.

This is the generation of competition. There was a time when you just had to compete with your neighbors over Christmas lights and tacky lawn ornaments. Now our newsfeeds flow with all the awesome philanthropy, money, and stardom our old college roommates have found, and then we look at our own lives and we feel like we don't measure up.

We give our children names such as Apple and Atticus because we wouldn't dare allow one other kid in their classes to have the same name as them. No offense, Emma and William. Our kids are an extension of us, and we are special. We are different. We are so happy and fabulous. Except that we are depressed.

Here is what I think is part of the problem: social media has made us self-centered. People who are actually other oriented don't spend hours cropping photos of themselves that they can throw on their interweb shrines. They just don't. We can talk about how much we love people or how passionate we are about the homeless, but if our iPhones are out of iCloud storage because we have two thousand photos of ourselves and our meals, we aren't compassionate. We just want people to think we are. And then hit Like.

In his book *The Lucifer Effect: Understanding How Good People Turn Evil*, Philip Zimbardo, the creator of the notorious Stanford prison experiment, essentially says that under the right circumstances, most people would do evil things. Want to know the main seed of nearly every evil act? Selfishness. The more self-centered we are, the more evil we are willing to become. Today, 71 percent of American adults think eighteen- to twenty-nine-year-old millennials are selfish.* Enter the selfie generation.

Isaiah 14:13 speaks of the fall of Satan by giving us a little more

---

* Nick Gillespie, "Millennials Are Selfish and Entitled, and Helicopter Parents Are to Blame," *Time*, August 21, 2014, http://time.com/3154186/millennials-selfish-entitled-helicopter-parenting/.

background information. It says this of the devil's fall:

> You said in your heart,
>   "I will ascend to the heavens;
> I will raise my throne
>   above the stars of God."

By the way, Satan is not the actual name for the devil. His name is Lucifer, which translates to "light bearer." We just call him *Satan*. The Hebrew word *satan* means "the adversary." Lucifer became the adversary, or accuser, of God when he decided he wanted a place to rule in opposition to God's government. They are currently battling for Earth. The devil's love of God and good and morality became eroded by his love for *self*. The light bearer became known as the prince of darkness. You see, self is the tiny black seed that chokes everything, even its host, if watered.

I feel like social media makes it almost impossible to not become an egomaniac. Studies show this generation is 40 percent less empathetic than the generation before.* Remember how racist and judgmental you feel like your parents are? Turns out, crazy aunt Beth cares more about other people than you do. Selfishness is the root of all evil. It's the breath of Satan. I'm not trying to have any common ground with the guardian of hell. No thanks. Pass on that. This should freak us out! Instead, we just tweet it, hoping people will think we actually read an article. We didn't. Just the headline. But we are super passionate about it now. AmIRight?

Christ's *entire* gospel message is about dying to yourself and living in Christ. Social media posts that center on me, selfies of me, snaps and chats of my every waking second are the complete opposite of that message. The Lucifer effect has fallen on all of us like the black plague.

Even in evolutionary logic, the tribe only continues if it maintains the goal of taking care of one another. Your brain is wired with hormones that

---

*Pamela Paul, "From Students, Less Kindness for Strangers?" *New York Times*, June 25, 2010, https://www.nytimes.com/2010/06/27/fashion/27StudiedEmpathy.html.

cause you to want to need people, because your biology knows that the pack goes extinct if all the members don't look out for one another. This is a basic human principle. I look out for you, and you look out for me. So what happens when I feel like I have to constantly look out for myself? I have anxiety (its rates have never been as high as they are today). I spend my energy focusing on myself—the same energy I could have spent being a productive member to the group.

I don't know what the answer is, but I do know that we have to get a grip. If the devil can't get you trapped in sin, he will get you trapped in self. We can't be the center of our own worlds, and yet we have pages dedicated to how funny we are, smart we are, and beautiful we are. If you don't think that makes us more selfish, then you are either lying or naive.

And so for the hundredth time last week, I deleted the Facebook app from my phone. Please pray for my willpower (I wish I were joking). I recognize that this doesn't make me Nelson Mandela, but I am hoping it helps me to be a little less Regina George (*Mean Girls*, 2004). Besides, I should be able to have dinner with my husband without comparing my thighs to that girl I disliked in high school.

Millennials are the most educated and diverse generation on the planet. I want to be able to use the fact that I am alive and a part of this awesome moment in Earth's history to focus on how I can make the world better. I don't want to live an entire life for photo ops and food pics.

I want my marriage to make me selfless. I want to make my husband's plate before I make my own. I want to embody Christ and service through the gift that is a Christian marriage. I am not the perfect wife. I have failed my husband, and I am naturally pretty selfish. But here is the beauty about walking with God: He changes you.

Bible Verse for Reflection
"I have been crucified with Christ and I no longer live, but Christ lives in me. The life I now live in the body, I live by faith in the Son of God, who loved me and gave himself for me" (Galatians 2:20).

Questions

- Today is not about you. Do all you can to serve your partner.
- What you are being selfish about in your life?
- How does focusing on self hurt a marriage?

Who Is Your Family?

Success in marriage does not come merely through finding the right mate, but through being the right mate.
—Barnett R. Brickner

The US Census Bureau defines *primary families* as two or more people who live together where members are related by birth, marriage, or adoption.* By this definition of *family*, the word covers those within our homes and excludes those outside of our homes. For most of us, however, that is simply too constricting. Our families are more than just those who live with us. Other definitions of *family* can include people we call family by choice; people who rely on each other for social, emotional, and/or financial support. Do you rely on your spouse to fulfill your social and emotional needs? That is part of the design.

How would Satan best strike the core of a race of people? It is my belief that his best war tactic would be to destroy marriage and its sanctity. To attack marriage—the root of the family—is to decimate the seed from which the family will grow. It is the very first institution God set into place for this world. Before the commandments, before the church, before every other religious institution, God created marriage. He created marriage as a union for us here on Earth, and the very next day He rested, thus creating a remembrance and reflection of His work on our behalf

---

* "Current Population Survey, Subject Definitions," United States Census Bureau, accessed October 2, 2018, https://www.census.gov/programs-surveys/cps/technical-documentation/subject -definitions.html#family.

and establishing our union and marriage to Him.

When you got married, you established a partnership with your mate. You decided that you would take on this world together, along with the suffering and joys it could bring. God knew that two were better than one. (See Ecclesiastes 4:9–12.) Where one may meet suffering and crumble, two could hold each other and stand. God knew that it would take the two of you to join forces and remain loyal to one another and that from that love and loyalty, children could be born or adopted in order to extend the love from the marriage unit to a family circle. When the foundation of marriage is strong, the family can prosper. In Bible times, families stayed together so long that they became tribes. Families are the system of checks and balances of our world. There is no love or loyalty quite like in a family. Families can hold each other accountable and together. They are pertinent to our edification.

I tell you this in the beginning to set the tone for the next twenty-eight days. You are married. I want you to understand how powerful this union is because I believe the world would have you forget. We are living in a world, and a country, in which marriage may still be fashionable, but "till death do you part" isn't. Loyalty is no longer a virtue in this individualistic society. The world and our media would have you believe that marriage and monogamy are old fashioned and outdated. Maybe if we spice marriage up, allow for multiple partners, divorce when we find someone else who gets whatever we're going through at the moment a little better than our spouse does, perhaps that would make marriage "cool" in the twenty-first century. Satan is out to destroy marriage, and the funny thing is, most of America doesn't even realize it. In fact, we're helping him!

Research shows that happily married people (especially men) are healthier, richer, and having better sex than single people.* Yes! Married people are having better sex than single people! Marriage is one of the

---

* W. Bradford Wilcox and Nicholas H. Wolfinger, "Men & Marriage: Debunking the Ball and Chain Myth," Institute for Family Studies, February 2017, https://ifstudies.org/wp -content/uploads/2017/02/IFSMenandMarriageResearchBrief2.pdf.

most fulfilling aspects of living on this earth. And yet, as many of us have gotten married to the wrong people and for the wrong reasons, we tarnish the beauty and fulfillment of marriage to those around us. Marriage is worth waiting for. It is worth praying for and certainly worth fighting for.

Everything God does is meticulous and intentional, and Christ's very first mission after creation was marriage. Satan was Christ's number one student. He has studied and learned and worked right alongside Jesus Christ and the Godhead. He has spent years learning from the brightest Intelligence in the entire universe. Do not underestimate Satan and his abilities. Not only has Satan been watching Christ, but he has spent thousands of years studying humanity. He knows that if he can succeed in destroying your marriage, he can also take out your family. We are no match; but with the help of Jesus Christ, we can overcome the temptations and seductions that Satan will bring right into the heart of our families.

My father has told me on countless occasions that a world with no more uncorrupted children (which is a world we are clearly nearing) is a world where grace can no longer reach. Once the purity and innocence of children can be infiltrated, Satan will have free reign as king of this earth. Because without good seed, what can be grown? You and your marriage are your child's best chance at prosperity. Our marriages are the pillars of our families. We have to take time to nurture these heavenly covenants.

Don't just tell your kids what love is; show them. Don't explain to your son how to be a man; show him how a real man treats his wife and protects his family. Don't discuss with your daughter how to love; be the kind of wife that is loyal to her husband and practices compassion with her children. Marriages have the power to give the greatest glory to God imaginable, producing righteous children that bring light to a world of darkness. Your marriage is sacred, and Satan is like a rabid dog, foaming at the mouth to tear it apart. It's not going to be easy, because he is going to make sure it's hard. But I can promise you one thing: if both you and your spouse want to use your marriage to God's glory, ask Him for guidance every single day. He will show up.

That last thing I cannot stress enough is that if you are not spending much time with God, you have to start devoting time to Him now. Let this next month together set the tone for the rest of this year, and the year after that, and the year after that. You must spend time with God daily. It's your only chance to develop the relationship with Him that will affect all your other relationships.

I cannot emphasize enough the ways in which your life will transform when you make time to meet God daily. He becomes real to you. You will see Him interact with you personally. You will hear His whisper even before you go looking for Him in the mornings. You have to seek His counsel as you allow yourself to grow as a husband or wife because without Him, you won't have a clue where to start. What's cool about God is that you don't have to devote your life to ministry; you don't have to become a missionary; you don't even have to figure out how to fix yourself. All you have to do is set aside time each day to commune with Christ alone. He does the rest.

Spend time in prayer each day and with Scripture each day. Take this relationship as you would any other relationship—one day at a time. Get to know Him, start dating Him, fall in love with Him, and marry Him! You can't allow either commitment to fall by the wayside.

This earthly marriage deserves your utmost tenderness and affection. This is not something you can set aside for later. This book will reflect on marriage and faith for the next several weeks, but my prayer is that these thirty-one days will simply be the beginning of the rest of your life. You have already made the biggest decision you will probably ever make. You got married. This book is about figuring out how to affirm the decision that you have already made in your marriage and in your faith. Allow me to pray for you before you go.

Dear Lord, I do not personally know the person who is reading these words, but I don't have to because You do. I ask, Lord, that You rock her to the core over these next few weeks and that You challenge her to pour love and tenderness over her spouse in such a way that a hedge grows around the marriage that not even Satan can penetrate. I ask that You allow the prayer written on her heart to be that You make her into the spouse You created her to be.

Remind her why she fell in love and of the vows she took. Let this person's life and marriage bring you glory and honor in an authentic display of Christianity. Amen.

Bible Verse for Reflection

"The LORD God said, 'It is not good for the man to be alone. I will make a helper suitable for him.' Now the LORD God had formed out of the ground all the wild animals and all the birds in the sky. He brought them to the man to see what he would name them; and whatever the man called each living creature, that was its name. So the man gave names to all the livestock, the birds in the sky and all the wild animals. But for Adam no suitable helper was found. So the LORD God caused the man to fall into a deep sleep; and while he was sleeping, he took one of the man's ribs and then closed up the place with flesh. Then the LORD God made a woman from the rib he had taken out of the man, and he brought her to the man" (Genesis 2:18–22).

Questions
- What is your definition of *family*?
- Who makes up your family?
- Reflect on what family members you listed and what family members you left out. Why did you make these choices?

This Moment in Marriage

*A successful marriage requires falling in love
many times, always with the same person.*
—Mignon McLaughlin

My husband and I went for a walk the other evening. We'd had a bit of an argument; I don't really remember what about, probably nothing, as most of the things we bicker about tend to go that way. I let him go by himself for a while. I stopped trying to work things out in the heat of the moment a long time ago. Now, if he is upset, I let him go. He's usually not gone long—a half hour to an hour at the most—but by the time he comes back, he's almost always more loving and softer with his words. When he came back home, he asked me to go for a walk, and so we did.

We walked a different route than usual. He held my hand, and I knew the argument didn't matter anymore. By the time we got to the place where we had planned to turn back, we decided to walk farther and enter the graveyard at the end of the road. The cemetery was filled with hundreds, if not thousands, of headstones. We started examining them. I ran my fingers over the smooth granite and traced the old letters engraved years before. Some of them were from the 1700s, and I was overwhelmed with awe at their beauty as well as with sadness for the lives that had once been vibrant and now had been silenced.

Row upon row, family name upon family name, lives were littered across this cemetery. Dreams had lived and died. Hopes had been born and crushed. I found myself imagining what the people may have been like. I was struck by the feeling of loss that must have echoed in their homes once they were gone. No matter who you are or what you've done, you can't help but feel completely insignificant when standing in a cemetery. I squeezed the hand of my husband and felt an ache in my soul as I realized again that this life is but a moment.

This book isn't about fixing your marriage; it's about affirming it. You see, we all have this one life—this one, tiny, insignificant life. Eventually, we will all join that bed in the ground where we will rest until we are called by our Savior. Once we are dead, all we have done, all the money we made, all the respect we earned, all the sweat of our brows will be forgotten; it will be silenced by our graves. All that we have, then, all that we can really hang our hats on in this world is the hope that one day everything you have done here will be acknowledged and you will be rewarded by Jesus Christ. One day the Lord of heaven and earth will call you by name and thank you for your service. Really, all we can do is live lives that bring Him glory and make Him proud.

I think this is important to recognize as a Christian but even more so as a married Christian couple. The second you decide as an individual to allow your own will to die and to give God complete control over your life, Satan will be waiting. He's a brilliant opponent who is completely aware of how short this life is. All he has to do is keep you busy, which doesn't even necessarily mean that you are busy with negative things. As long as you are occupied with anything that is not God's plan for your life, he knows he can win. Your mate needs your encouragement to keep focused just as much as you need his or hers. You must remember that your marriage is not just meant for your happiness but is a holy union formed by God. You can achieve your earthly mission with the affirmation of one another. Put the other before yourself, and there's no way you can lose.

A thought crossed my mind this morning. I wondered, *What if I make it? What if I stay the course, keep the faith, and go to heaven? What if I get there and meet with Jesus face-to-face? What if, when I'm there, He holds my gaze and says, "You did good, but had you listened every time I called, here's what you could have done," or "Here's who else could have been here"?*

I think sometimes we get comfortable with the idea that we are being good, and we forget that we were created in the image of Jesus Christ, which means that "good" doesn't even scratch the surface.

I am convinced that this world is dying. I am convinced that time is winding down and that the battle of good versus evil on this earth is about to have a victor. Unlike other things I've written or the thousands of other times I have sat down to put my thoughts on paper, I am completely burdened with the idea that we as Christians have to rally and do everything in our power to answer His call. I don't want to go to heaven and hear that I missed a single word of a message that He knew only I could deliver. I don't want to just barely make it. I want to exceed His expectations. The stakes are just too high to leave any rock unturned.

You're married. You have a head start in this whole thing, if you ask me. Your marriage is quite possibly what could propel you to greatness. Not only is God in heaven rooting for your success, but you also have an earthly partner whom you can confide in and who can verbally affirm you every single day. God brought you together to speak love to each other on His behalf. You are incredibly lucky, and Satan is incredibly weakened the second the two of you get on the same page.

Our lives may end up like the billions before us. From dust we were created and to dust we shall return. One thing I take extreme heart in, though, is that come resurrection morning, after all the sweat, tears, and heartbreak I will have endured in this life, I will wake up right beside my lover, my partner, and my best friend. You see, the only thing sweeter than finishing the toughest race is finishing it alongside the person you love. So why not love your spouse right here, right now, today. This life is but a moment.

Bible Verse for Reflection

"Do nothing out of selfish ambition or vain conceit. Rather, in humility value others above yourselves, not looking to your own interests but each of you to the interests of the others. In your relationships with one another, have the same mindset as Christ Jesus" (Philippians 2:3–5).

Questions

- How can you take a moment today to show your partner that he or she matters?
- What is one word of encouragement you can give your partner before the day is over?
- Why are you lucky to have married your partner?

A Letter to My Exes

Nobody deserves your tears, but whoever
deserves them will not make you cry.
—Gabriel García Márquez

To the kid who used to chase me around at day care: I never knew what to expect other than I would be afraid to be without my parents. Eventually, I would have another thing that I could count on: you chasing me. All the kids would be playing in the makeshift playground the babysitter had created in her backyard. I can remember looking for toads with a friend and daring each other to kiss one and see if it turned into a prince. Somewhere in between picking dandelions and toad kissing, your mom would drop you off. Within minutes, you would survey the area and then decide to chase me. I am not sure if you thoroughly enjoyed playing tag and were obsessed with being "it" or if you just loved chasing me. Either way, I ran. You never could catch me, and that made you chase me more. Thank you for teaching me that it works well when the boy chases the girl and that boys like girls who aren't caught too quickly.

To the boy in first grade who passed me the note: I didn't mean to hurt you. I was sitting in class trying desperately to master those tricky times tables when your note was handed down our row and landed on my desk. "To Heather," it said in block letters. "Top Secret." I looked down the row and knew who had sent it before I read the signature. You had buried your face in your math book, and your tapping foot revealed your nerves. "Do you like me? Circle yes or no." I circled no and handed it back down the

25

line. I didn't even feel bad when I saw you read my reply and then crinkle the paper into a ball in your pocket. I didn't keep it "top secret" either, and for that, I am sorry. I can remember one of my friends laughing and pointing while you walked by. You wore green corduroy pants, and your glasses looked foggy. I want you to know that I would go on to receive my own rejections. You taught me that life will hand all of us our fair share of nos.

To the boys in my sixth-grade class: You made a list of the prettiest girls in the classroom almost weekly and posted it on the girls' bathroom door. I would have given anything to see my name ranked first on that list for just one day. I never did. There were days I was terrified to go to school. I was scared to see that dreaded list and where my name would fall. You taught all the girls a lesson I wish I could have forgotten: boys want girls to be pretty. I spent a great deal of my time focusing my energy in the wrong places because of that stupid list. I didn't care if I was smart; I didn't care if I was funny; I didn't care if I had a scholarship. I just wanted the boys to think I was pretty. Thank you (*not!*) for encouraging me to waste so much of my youth sizing up all the other girls in the room.

To the boy who didn't stay long: You always had to be perfect. I am not sure I ever saw a hair out of place or an outfit without matching shoes. Your parents had an incredible house, and you had the coolest car. You'd tell me about the scholarships you were offered, but your stories were as fake as your promises. You were the boy all my friends warned me about. The boy even *your* friends warned me about. You were the life of the party. We'd make plans for a group of us to meet at the movies. I'd spend hours getting ready. I didn't mind the big crowds because I wanted everyone to see that you were with me. Looking back, I am not sure anyone could have even known you were there with me. You gave so many girls such special attention. We'd talk in the lobby after, and I can remember wishing that time would stand still. It never did, and you always had somewhere else to rush off to. You never could stay long. You taught me a lesson I should have learned immediately: boys like you don't stay long.

26

A Letter to My Exes

To my "best friend" in high school: You were my first phone call when I failed my parking test for driver's ed. You told me that I'd be a licensed Michigan driver, and you'd make sure of it! You spent the rest of that weekend driving around stealing those orange construction cones. You picked me up on Sunday evening and told me you had a surprise for me. I got into your big truck that always made me feel so small, and we drove to an empty parking lot. You had set the cones up just like the parking garage. You smiled at me and, without saying a word, unbuckled your seat belt and got out of the driver's side so that I could practice my parallel parking. You were so proud when I passed that test. On cold winter nights when the rest of our friends were out partying, you'd beg me to drive aimlessly around town looking at Christmas lights. I realize now how much effort you put into keeping me right where you wanted me. I remember your mom telling me once that I was so pretty; but while she was talking, her face revealed pity. I felt special, and she felt sorry for me. I'd sit and force a smile while you'd tell me about the girl you were in love with that week. I'd even help you think of romantic dates or nice gestures you could do to surprise every girl that wasn't me. For four years, I wanted to be more than just your best friend, and for four years, you pretended like you hadn't noticed. In college, you called me one night and cried. You told me that you realized how foolish you had been. You said that we were soul mates and that you hoped it wasn't too late. It was. You taught me that the boy I wanted to be with wouldn't spend our time together talking about other girls. I learned that people will go to great lengths to keep you within their reach and that orange construction cones and Christmas lights were how you said "I'm sorry."

To the first boy who said "I love you": You'd drive an hour and a half just to put a rose on my car and tap on my window. I'd whisper that you were crazy, but I was obviously thrilled. You gave me extravagant gifts and always made me your number one priority. You were a gentleman. You were kind and thoughtful, and for a long time, I thought I'd only ever have one boyfriend. Life never felt real with you because we never had any problems. Money was no issue, time was no issue, other girls were never an issue. I knew if I married you, I'd have adventurous vacations, shopping extravaganzas, and date nights where we could do whatever I wanted. But you taught me, perhaps, the most valuable lesson I would ever learn: though I could build a relationship off of attraction, kindness, dreams, or even love, it was better to build it on a shared faith. You taught me that I wanted something magical with Christ even more than I wanted something magical with a boy. I never again dated a boy with whom I couldn't experience God. I learned that from you.

To the "bad boy" I wanted so badly my freshman year of college: I can still remember the first moment I saw you. You were standing in the gym, and I whispered to the girl next to me, "Who's he?" She responded, "Bad news." They warned me, but I didn't listen. I thought I would be different. I thought I could change you. My father told me not to believe the things that boys say but instead to watch their actions. Even so, I couldn't stop hanging on your every word. I wanted to believe you. You broke my heart one day in July and then just drove away. I stood there watching your car pull away. I saw smoke come from your car's exhaust, but what I wanted to see was remorse. I kept hoping I'd see you look back. You didn't. I learned that day that boys like you don't look back.

To the boy that I left: In my mind, you are sitting on the old wooden bench in front of my parents' house and you're crying. You keep repeating yourself, but I am mostly numb. I wasn't good to you, and to be honest, I hope you did better. A lot of things were right with us, but one big thing was wrong: I didn't love you. Finally, I understood how the boy who never stayed long and the one who didn't look back did it. They didn't love me. I know now that real love stays long and that even when you leave it, you keep one eye trained on your rearview mirror. You taught me that you can't force yourself to feel something and that I wanted to be crazy about the next boy I let hold my hand. The other boys taught me to live life more cautiously, but you taught me that I would be happier if I just jumped in. You taught me not to let fear hold me back or to let ease make me settle. I wanted to fall passionately in love, and maybe I never would have let myself had I not learned that from you.

A Letter to My Exes

To my husband: I had never had someone swallow me with affection like you did. I can remember the first time you kissed me. I was talking about how I wanted to be a writer and how I had just submitted my first book for publication. While I was in the middle of my sentence, you kissed me. I always thought someone should ask permission before doing something like that, but I don't think boys who looked like you ever had to ask for much of anything. On Christmas Eve 2010, you proposed to me. Your mother had told me the summer before that she didn't think you'd ever commit to anyone. Despite all the lessons I had already learned, my gut told me she was wrong. You had me opening about fifteen presents in my one-bedroom apartment. You were smiling so brightly, and I remember thinking that I had never seen a more perfect face. You handed me the last gift, and when it was opened, I forced a smile. It was a book—an old, classic literary work. You knew I loved writing and reading. I figured you were trying to be sweet, but I have never read *A Tale of Two Cities* or anything by Faulkner. Classics aren't my style. You lowered your head and said, "You don't like it, do you?" I tried harder to make my smile appear genuine. "It's a special book," you said. "You have to read it a little different." You took it from me and started flipping the pages slowly, like how my mom used to when I was a kid and she wanted to show me how the once-standing-still man could run. "Will You Marry Me?" flashed across a thousand pages; and in the back of the book, a hole had been carved for a ring.

Seth, I wrote this because there are so many days that I find myself wishing it had been you all along. I wasted so much time and so many tears over boys that would never come close to being what you've been to me. But then I realized there is more than one way to write a fairy tale and that every experience has taught me how lucky I am. I can't change my past, but I can let my past help direct my future. I think I did that, and I think that's how I found you. I'll stop wishing now and just be grateful that I found the boy who always looks back, who always stays, and who puts my name at the very top of his "pretty" list.

Most important, I found a boy with whom I could share my faith and whose belief could lift me up in the moments when I can't breathe. You are a reminder that God writes love stories. Marriage is the very first institution God ever made. He is a champion of marriage and wants to be involved in the dating and relationship choices we make that lead us to that celebration. Your history is not your destiny, and I wish I had consulted God before I ever went on my first date.

I love you, my dear husband, and I realized as I wrote this that I've been learning to love you all along.

Bible Verse for Reflection

"Let your eyes look straight ahead; fix your gaze directly before you" (Proverbs 4:25).

Questions

- How has your past led you to your future?
- Can you see God's hand leading you to your marriage?
- In what ways do you believe God brought your marriage together?

I Don't Have a Happy Marriage

The best friend will probably acquire the best wife,
because a good marriage is founded on the talent for friendship.
—Friedrich Nietzsche

Last week I chugged a caramel mocha, heavy on the whipped cream. When I raised my eyes from my cup, I saw my husband grinning at me.

"Are you happy?" he asked.

He has asked me this question a hundred times before. I don't know why this is the first time I actually heard it. It was as if, for the first time, it clicked with me how often my husband checks in to make sure I am enjoying whatever activity we are doing. "Are you happy?" is like his tag line. It doesn't matter where we are or what stage of life we are in. On our first date, we sat at the beach and dangled our feet off the pier while watching the sunset. "Are you happy?" he whispered in my ear.

He has been asking me this question for nearly a decade; yet two weeks ago in that little coffee shop was the first time I really heard it.

My husband wants to make my life better. He actively tries to find ways to make sure he is measurably doing that. When I'm not happy, we fix it. We switch restaurants; we spend more time together; we put the kids in the car and go for a drive. His philosophy is, if we aren't happy, let's do something different and see if it helps. But you can't change what you don't acknowledge. Sometimes I don't even realize I am happy until he asks me. I'm face deep in whipped cream and caramel. This is exhilarating.

Thanks for making me pause long enough to notice.

I'm not easy to make happy either. I mean, chips and salsa aside, I am a complex social creature. I'm one of those all-in personalities. I am either living THE BEST LIFE EVER (caps necessary), or I'm sobbing in the dark, wailing to the wind that God has forgotten me. I believe the clinical term for this is *manic*. For the sake of my tender ego, we will go with *flaky*, because I am pretty sure that's not technically a mental illness. Nonetheless, it's important to take stock of where you are and to let yourself put words to it. Are you happy? In your job, in your home, in your marriage, in your body? Are you truly happy? Or are you just busy? There is a difference.

We tend to think that life is something that happens to us rather than something we are supposed to make happen for ourselves. It's OK if you aren't happy. We are the first generation to be able to binge-watch *Grey's Anatomy* seasons one through ninety-seven in a four-day blackout. Some of us aren't used to hard work and things that don't come quickly. We want microwaves and Hulu. Our idea of patience is watching Super Bowl commercials. Of course, no one thinks they have the magical, romantic marriage their Instagram friends do. Of course, we all question our own career choices, relationship choices, and parenting choices. These things take time and work to filter through, and we aren't used to that.

I teach communications, and one thing that has always fascinated me is how prone relationships are to conflict. The tighter the relationship, the greater the number of conflicts. What that means is that marriage is filled with discord, and that's normal. It doesn't mean you have an unhappy marriage; it means you are highly dependent on another person and that often creates points of contention. Of course, you and your best pals aren't experiencing conflict. You aren't lying next to them at 3:00 A.M., contemplating your own death (or theirs) due to their noisy breathing. This marriage junk is far more complex than the word *happy* can even begin to unravel. Some nights you get the warm fuzzies watching your spouse sleep; and others you are huddled under the covers, searching the interwebs for one-way flights to Taiwan. That's life, homey. Peaks and valleys.

I don't have a happy marriage. No one does. *Happy* doesn't even begin to scratch the surface of the highs and lows that come with devotion and commitment. What we do have are complex relationships with people who, we hope, try to make our lives better, even when they don't know how.

And honestly, doesn't that make you happy?

Bible Verse for Reflection
"He who finds a wife finds what is good and receives favor from the LORD" (Proverbs 18:22).

Questions
- How would you describe your marriage?
- What makes your spouse happy?
- Think of a small gesture you can perform to bring your spouse happiness today.

Churched Out

*The perfect church service would be one we were almost
unaware of; our attention would have been on God.*
—C. S. Lewis

I was having a conversation with a friend a couple of months ago. She
was struggling with actually attending church. "I just don't see why I
need it," she said.

I wanted to prove to her that she did need church. I wanted to convince
her that the church was a safe place where she could get direction and
peace from people who care about her development. I wanted to fight for
the value of investing in a relationship with the church in the same way
I am able to fight for the value of investing in a relationship with God. I
instantly wished the church looked more like the Jesus I knew. Instead, I
took a bite of my sandwich.

Church-attendance numbers among millennials are the lowest they
have been in history. Only two out of ten Americans under thirty say
attending church is worthwhile. Fifty-nine percent of the millennials
that grew up in church won't go back, and 35 percent hold an "anti-
church stance."[*] Next time you go to church, look around the pews.
Odds are your youth group isn't there with you. What baffles me about
this is that the church just keeps going on like it's business as usual.

---

[*] "Americans Divided on the Importance of Church," Barna Group, March 24, 2014, https://
www.barna.com/research/americans-divided-on-the-importance-of-church/.

But it's not. Young people aren't buying what the church is selling, and I have spent the last few months trying to figure out why I couldn't explain to my friend all the ways that the church would be able to make her life better.

I struggle with "the church." I recognize that every church is different, so I am talking in generalities about some of the people that ruin church for the rest of us. In fact, I struggle with that. We always shift blame on to someone else. Whispering that my generation is just "not spiritual" sounds ridiculous when I look at the philanthropy work of many of my millennial friends. I thank God that He made human beings with hearts like that. Some of them aren't even Christians. You don't have to be searching for God in order for Him to come looking for you or to work through you. I don't believe millennials are rejecting God as much as they are rejecting the church's representation of Him. And on most weekends, can you blame them?

I struggle with the finger-pointing many in our churches do when it comes to sin. I struggle with people who think that sin is just meth addiction and porn binges. The church taught me a lot about being wary of the dark voodoo of sin, which I find ironic, because the church seems to love sin so much. Sin isn't just getting drunk in high school and having sex in the back seat of cars, but that's all I heard about in chapel. In a lot of ways, I think sin is much more vicious than that, because breaking the spirit of God's law is even easier than breaking the letter of the law.

Sin is ungrateful hearts and exclusive words. It's posting videos of ourselves feeding the homeless because we care more about followers than poor people. It's doing good deeds for a profit margin. Sin is looking the other way when you notice scars on the arms of the kid in the grocery store. It's greed. It's posting memes that insult other races. Sin is saying you love your neighbors while refusing to leave your own neighborhood. It's screaming insults at teenage girls entering abortion clinics and *not* screaming at the systems that produce teenage girls who think they need abortions. It's the fact that as of 2016, there were more than 430,000 children in the US foster care system,* and in this same country in 2014, more than 170 million people identified as Christians.† You do the math.

Sin is telling girls that the way they were dressed they were "asking to be raped." Sexual assault is all over our schools, our workplaces, and our neighborhoods. It is making a mockery of our churches too. I personally know women who have been victimized by every single adult male they have ever come across in their entire lives. So yes, they struggle with connecting to your male pastor.

There are people right here in this country who never had parents who were sober enough to tuck them in at night. They have burns on their arms from cigarette butts extinguished on them by their own mothers. Their own fathers rob their piggy banks. They don't know how to dream because they've never felt safe enough to let their minds wander—and you don't understand why it's hard for them to believe in a loving God? Sin is not just prostitution and murder. It's being so consumed with yourself that even while the world is burning down around you, you have the stomach to argue about politics.

I think more millennials would be in church if churches held more honest people. We dress nice and look pretty, smile all the smiles, and promise not to cuss. But what we really need is a place where some real people, who have been through some real stuff, can tell us stories about a real God and how they met Him personally. That's a gospel we would buy into.

I read a tweet the other day that reminded me of why I still follow pastors on Twitter. "People don't want a church," it said. "They want a family." I have a handful of people who aren't related to me by blood who I know I can call in the middle of the night from a bed soaked in tears, and they'd sit with me in the dark. I can pray with them, I can show my

---

* "The AFCARS Report," U.S. Department of Health and Human Services, accessed September 11, 2018, https://www.acf.hhs.gov/sites/default/files/cb/afcarsreport24.pdf.

† Becka A. Alper and Aleksandra Sandstrom, "If the U.S. Had 100 People: Charting Americans' Religious Affiliations," Pew Research Center, November 14, 2016, http://www.pewresearch.org/fact-tank/2016/11/14/if-the-u-s-had-100-people-charting-americans-religious-affiliations.

sins to them, and they will walk me off the ledge. They are the church I want to go to. That's the kind of church I could fight for.

Since the beginning of the human experience, Satan has been hell bent on luring human beings into sins so grotesque that he believes Christ wouldn't see them as worthy of fighting for. The church abused Christ's body. They worked tirelessly to destroy His ministry. Eventually, they tore His skin, pierced His hands, and broke His heart. Christ fights for them anyway. The same church that murdered Him He found worthy to die for. So while I have days where I feel churched out, I recognize that there is something buried in that community that I can't just walk away from. I can try to be the church for someone else that others refused to be for me.

The next time a friend asks me why she needs church, I'm just going to be honest. "Maybe you don't need church," I'll say, "but I do know the church needs you."

And then I'll take a bite of my sandwich.

Bible Verse for Reflection

"Built on the foundation of the apostles and prophets, Christ Jesus himself being the cornerstone, in whom the whole structure, being joined together, grows into a holy temple in the Lord. In him you also are being built together into a dwelling place for God by the Spirit" (Ephesians 2:20–22, ESV).

Questions
- What do you like about your current church?
- How are you being the church for someone else?
- Why may we need the church?

Can Wives Lead at Church Too?

"What women these Christians have!"
—Libanius

I am an academic. In academia, you can be a lot of things as long as Christian isn't one of them. At the college I worked for prior to Andrews University, I had a colleague ask me quite candidly why I would ever attach myself to a religion that belittles my position in the community based on my gender. He wasn't being rude. He was genuinely concerned for my psyche.

During the last year, I have been asking myself the same question. Does the Bible place women in an inferior role to men? Is God sexist? Can I be a Christian and believe that men and women have an equal calling in ministry? And if so, why are so many people telling me no?

I have heard Christian men express opinions that certainly sound as if God is sexist. While they would never call Him sexist, they just make statements that certainly sound like God prefers men over women—see what I did there?

"Due to sin," they'll say, "women are simply lower on the totem pole than their male counterparts." I have also heard Christian women say that they would never vote for a woman in political office, or really in any position of authority, if there were a suitable man to fill that same role. God established the hierarchy; don't shoot the messenger. But did He? And is this *mansplaining* biblical?

In ancient Israel, the right to the priesthood was not available to those who felt called to ministry as it is today. The right was strictly reserved for a group of the Levite tribe—namely, the descendants of Aaron as found in Exodus 28:41.

The priesthood of ancient Israel had three primary duties:

1. Administration
2. Prophecy
3. Sacrifices and dealing with the services in the temple

By looking at these three functions, we have biblical evidences of women in Israel performing two of the three duties. Women did serve as judges and administrators; the best example, of course, is Deborah, who was not only a spiritual judge for Israel but also a military strategist on equal footing with Barak, the male general.

We see examples of women prophesying and read references in Joel and Acts of women prophesying. From this, we see that the only function barred to women, and excluding them from the priesthood, was the practice of sacrificial rites, though we do see women preparing sacrificial meals, and they were present at the ceremonies.

The Bible offers no explanation as to why women were not able to perform sacrifices, but I don't believe this excludes women in today's age, considering that the Lamb has been slain and no further ceremonial practices regarding sacrifice take place.

Is there actual biblical evidence of God wanting to use women too? I believe I am theologically safe to be both a Christian and a feminist. If you'll give me a few minutes, I'd like to tell you why.

People always say that Eve was created to be Adam's "helpmate," but this is a difficult term to translate into English. In my research for my book *Life After Eden*, I discovered that the Hebrew word used by God in our Genesis passage on helpmates is *Ezer*. This is the same term seen in 1 Samuel 7 when Samuel raises his "Eben*ezer*."

It is in the Old Testament that we gain further understanding of what it means to "raise my Ebenezer." In 1 Samuel 7, we read that the Israelites were under attack from the Philistines. Outnumbered and in fear for their lives, they pled with the prophet Samuel to pray for God's help. Samuel offered a sacrifice and prayed for protection. In response, the Lord smote the Philistines, and they retreated to their territory. This victory is recorded in verse 12: "Then Samuel took a stone and set it up between Mizpah and Shen. He named it Ebenezer, saying, 'Thus far the LORD has helped us.' "

Ezer is a masculine noun in Hebrew and appears twenty-one times in the Old Testament. Most of those instances refer to help from someone stronger.

Eve was to be the helpmate of Adam, and together they would be equals. Together, Adam would be made stronger. Eve was created to make Eden stronger, the earth stronger, and our social bonds stronger. God made Eve and said she shall make Adam stronger. God loves women. He thinks we make things strong.

Can I be a Christian and a feminist? All I know is that God knew Adam would need strength to thwart that crafty devil, and so He gave him a woman. How terrible then, that the person who was to be Adam's equal, who was to make him stronger, enticed him into sin. Eve failed her husband. But I think her daughters can help restore God's plan.

Women were created to make this world a better place. God created woman and called her *Ezer* with the intention that she would help make the people and things around her stronger. Don't tell me that God is misogynistic. He made women to be strong, not weak. Don't tell me that God doesn't have a plan for His female creation. He created woman with a purpose. He designed her to fulfill a specific role in Eden and a specific role in these last days. Eve may have failed, but we better not.

God loves restoration—He is all about restoration. Take a look at the Scriptures and you'll soon see that everything He touches gets restored. He created a woman to make this world stronger and she failed. As the daughters of Eve, we share in the painful swallow of that first bite of sin in Eden.

Eve may have failed. Her daughters better not.

Bible Verse for Reflections

"Our daughters will be like pillars carved to adorn a palace" (Psalm 144:12).

Questions

- Do you feel like women are pillars in the areas they serve?
- Has someone ever told you that God values women less than men? How did that make you feel?
- How can you be a pillar in your church?

Don't Let Your Kids Ruin Your Marriage

*We do not develop habits of genuine love automatically. We learn
them by watching effective role models—most specifically by observing
how our parents express love for each other day in and day out.*
—Josh McDowell

A huge struggle in marriage begins the second you get pregnant. Immediately, women start fawning over these tiny humans. We talk to them; we play them music. We rub our bellies and hope they feel connected to the touch of our hands. Then we look at our husbands, and we wonder if we will ever love them like that.

I'm not saying all women do this, just most of us. We obsess over every grin, step, and fart and leave our husbands in the dust. Honestly, can you imagine the whiplash we give them? One minute we're asking for every detail of their day, and the next we don't even notice what time they came home.

Here is the thing about men: when they love, they love hard. We always credit women with being the primary lovers, but that's not necessarily true. Men love their wives and covet their affection. They desperately want you to laugh at their jokes, comment on their good looks, and show them some romance. Sometimes, new moms are too busy snapping selfies with their children to notice or are too tired.

In 1989, Susan Sprecher and Sandra Metts released research on what they called the "Romantic Beliefs Scale." Their study found that "men were generally more romantic than women."* "Men are more likely than women to believe in love at first sight, in love as the basis for marriage and for overcoming obstacles, and to believe that their partner and relationship will be perfect."† As relationships develop, men tend to become *more* romantic and women *less* romantic. Men also dream more about their lost partners after breakups as well as spend more time fantasizing than women. When it comes to love, men don't settle. Men's biological clock continues ticking a bit longer than women's, so they don't generally feel the need to rush.

The odds are that a man who marries you is a man who is desperately in love with you. He knew it the second he saw you, and he falls more in love with you each day. The issue here is that men have a really difficult time communicating how they feel. In general, men tend to have a harder time expressing themselves than women do. Women are great at building relationships. We tell our friends how we feel. I say, "I love you" before hanging up with most of my girlfriends. He doesn't do that. It doesn't come as natural for him, but that doesn't mean he doesn't feel it.

Ask a happily married man if he would die for his wife. Without hesitation, he will say yes. Ask a woman if she would die for her husband. She will probably ask you fifty other questions; one of which is probably, "But why are we dying?"

Marilyn Montgomery and Gwendolyn Sorell found in their 1998 study on adolescent romance that "boys fell in love earlier and more often than girls."‡ Researchers asked college students from eleven different countries the question, "If a man (woman) had all the other qualities desired, would you marry this person if you were not in love with him (her)?" A higher percentage of males responded no, indicating that men are highly

---

* Susan Sprecher and Sandra Metts, "Development of the 'Romantic Beliefs Scale' and Examination of the Effects of Gender and Gender-Role Orientation," *Journal of Social and Personal Relationships* 16, no. 6 (November 1989): 387–411, https://doi.org/10.1177/0265407589064001.

† Sprecher and Metts, "Development of the 'Romantic Beliefs Scale,'" 387–411.

‡ Marilyn Montgomery and Gwendolyn Sorell, "Love and Dating Experience in Early and Middle Adolescence: Grade and Gender Comparisons," *Journal of Adolescence* 21, no. 6 (December 1998): 677–689, http://doi.org/10.1006/jado.1998.0188.

concerned with the need for love and romance in a marriage.

A smaller percentage of women responded no, indicating that women will get married for a variety of reasons, and love doesn't have to be one of them.* Some women will maintain a relationship because a man makes a lot of money or he would be a really good dad.

But once a woman has a baby, suddenly she can't stop texting the daily rundown of what the baby did at breakfast. I mean that's sweet and all, but your husband still wants you too. You are more beautiful as a mother, but that doesn't mean he wants you to stop being a wife.

Don't let your kids ruin your marriage. Don't stop noticing his haircut or how funny he is around his friends. Don't stop showing him you are attracted to him and asking him about his goals. Keep telling him your secrets, and build intimacy outside of your kids.

Men need that. And women actually need that too.

Bible Verse for Reflection

"Wives, submit to your own husbands, as to the Lord. For the husband is the head of the wife even as Christ is the head of the church, his body, and is himself its Savior. Now as the church submits to Christ, so also wives should submit in everything to their husbands" (Ephesians 5:22–24, ESV).

Questions

- What do you think it means to submit to your husband biblically?
- Do you feel like your marriage is the same today as when you first got married? What is better, and what is worse?
- What can you do today to be more intentional about creating a connection with your partner?

---

* Robert Levine, Suguru Sato, Tsukasa Hashimoto, Jyoti Verma, "Love and Marriage in Eleven Cultures," *Journal of Cross-Cultural Psychology* 26, no. 5 (September 1995): 554–571, http://journals.sagepub.com/doi/10.1177/0022022195265007.

DAY 10

God Doesn't Care Who You Marry

I have known many happy marriages, but never a compatible one.
The whole aim of marriage is to fight through and survive the
instant when incompatibility becomes unquestionable.
—G. K. Chesterton

I was twenty-one years old when I got engaged. I was ecstatic. I was twenty-two when I called off that same engagement, just two months before the wedding. I was devastated.

The day that my engagement ended was probably the worst day of my entire life. The stuff leading up to this decision kind of came out of nowhere. Our relationship wasn't perfect, or even healthy, but up until the exact moment that it ended, the thought that I may not actually marry him didn't enter my mind. I'd had a conversation with my parents in which they expressed concerns about the upcoming nuptials. When I thought about it, I realized that I had some concerns as well.

I knew I was too much of a coward to call it off on my own if that was what needed to be done, and so I prayed and said something like this, "Lord, this is the person that I have chosen; but if he isn't the person that You have chosen for me, please end it."

I am not kidding you: within two minutes of my saying "amen," my phone rang. It was my amazing, and yet not all that amazing, fiancé. He was breaking up with me. Now I should tell you that we did break up on a regular basis. "Break up to make up" had kind of been our norm. But we had not argued this day, we hadn't even disagreed. We even picked out

45

wedding invitations. Paid for them in real sweat equity, and suddenly he was breaking up with me. I should have asked for the receipt.

This was not a coincidence. I knew, without a doubt, that God had answered my prayer. I had always known that I should be careful what I asked God to intercede on and that I couldn't go all willy-nilly praying for Him to close doors I wasn't ready to see slam. But here I was, dumped, two months before my wedding.

I laid lifeless in my bed that evening. My parents had gone out of town, and I didn't have the strength to tell them what had happened yet. I hadn't even called any of my friends because they were either in my wedding or were his friends too. I was humiliated, and I could swear that the wedding dress hanging in my closet kept poking its head out and laughing at me.

I cast one more prayer to the Big Guy; this time asking for mercy. I was struggling to breathe in my twin-size bed. I needed peace. Again, my phone rang. I figured it was my fiancé calling to tell me that he was sorry. I needed his apology in order to keep my heart pumping, but I also knew that I still wasn't supposed to marry him.

I answered my phone, and the voice on the other end was not my fiancé's at all. It was Seth Day. I had met Seth in the sixth grade; I thought he was a total babe. He was small and tan with blue eyes. He would pass me notes, and I would save them. If I could have sprung for a laminator at eleven, I would have made that crinkled paper with scribbles timeless art. I can remember sitting in my room, folding and unfolding those notes, smiling each time I read his words.

"Lunch was gross today," he'd write, and I would play music behind his words.

His family moved away after our seventh grade, and I never saw him again. I was in my sophomore year of college when I laid eyes on him for the first time as an adult. I wrote my number down on a piece of paper and handed it to him. I waited for my note back. Just like old times, except now there was Google and I knew how to spell *laminator*.

I waited and waited and waited. He never wrote me or called me. Not even a wrong number. Later I saw him walking on campus with a girl who was apparently his girlfriend. I was slightly embarrassed, but I collected the fragments of my dignity and cast a half smile in his direction and waved my hand.

He smiled and waved in front of his pretty, little blond girlfriend. He was being friendly; I was being a masochist. I continued doing this for the rest of the semester, and periodically, when we would run into each other, he would ask questions about my life. We laughed about sixth grade, and the more I saw him, the less fake my smiles became.

Eventually, I started dating the guy who would later become my fiancé, and my crush on Seth faded. I had found the man I would marry, and it wasn't the boy I had written about in my sixth-grade diary. That was OK because life isn't a fairy tale.

You can imagine my disbelief when my phone rang, two years later, on the very night that I had prayed to God to intercede for me. Seth had saved my little piece of paper. He folded it and tucked it into his back-pack. It sat there for two years in mint condition, even without a lami-nator. He and his girlfriend had broken up a year earlier. He would later tell me that there were many days he had taken out that folded paper and started to dial my number, but he remembered the last time we talked, my gushing over my new boyfriend, and figured it was inappropriate. But he never threw away the note.

So here I am, on the very night that my fiancé and I break up, sobbing alone with God, half thanking Him, half hating Him for interceding in my life way too abruptly, and then my phone rings. I can still hear his voice, "Heather . . . Hey, I'm not really sure why I am calling. I just felt like I should."

Two years later, there was a wedding, not to my first fiancé but to the scrawny kid from sixth grade whom I'd scribbled diary notes about. God did give me a fairy tale. It just came wrapped in closed doors, fake smiles, and sleepless nights.

We have been married seven years. In between then and now, much has changed about this fairy tale. Romance stopped being candlelit din-ners and walks on the beach the moment I gave birth to our daughter.

Romance no longer meant new dresses and high heels. Somehow, after seven years of marriage, it has morphed into this new sense of intimacy. Somewhere in between dirty diapers at 2:00 A.M. and a stack of bills on the counter, romance became something different.

Romance looks a lot like cold pizza at breakfast and assembling baby cribs. It sounds like him starting the coffee first and knowing exactly how much creamer to give me. It feels like running to the store at midnight because we are out of milk. From my view, romance sounds like whispers during naptime and looks like macaroni cards. It's staying committed despite imperfection.

People complain that marriage sucks the romance out of relationships, and I couldn't disagree more. Marriage gives birth to a different phase of romance. The kind that isn't just fleeting hopes and sweaty palms. Romance has become something far more valuable than that. It has become something that only time and struggle can give birth to.

I always read blogs and articles from people who say God doesn't care who you marry, you just have to make a good choice. Nothing sends my fingers pounding a keyboard more quickly. If there is one thing I know for certain, it's that God *absolutely* cares about who you marry! There will be no earthly decision you will ever make that will affect the course of your life more than the choice of who you marry. I would not be who I am today if it were not for Seth's impact on my character. I would like to think that I would have become the woman I am regardless of who I married. But that would be a lie. Seth has taught me to think before I talk, to be honest even when I don't want to, and to love people because they are human rather than because of what they can do for me.

I had a professor once who said that when it comes to marriage, if you get that one aspect of your life wrong, everything else can go right, and none of it will matter. Likewise, if you get that one aspect of your life right, everything else can go wrong, and none of it will matter. He was right. A lot has gone wrong in these past seven years, and yet, somehow, none of that really matters.

If we say that God cares about the job you get or the school you attend or that He implanted so-and-so into your life to be a friend through a difficult time, how in the world could that same God not care about who you marry?

I was two months away from marrying the wrong man. I prayed a prayer at two o'clock in the morning, and *boom!* everything I thought I knew, I didn't. If God doesn't care about who we marry, the biggest life decision we can ever make, what exactly does this impersonal God care about?

I thought my life was ending the night that I called off my wedding. Then I discovered that with God and marriage, endings can look a lot like beginnings.

Bible Verse for Reflection

"For it is God who works in you to will and to act in order to fulfill his good purpose" (Philippians 2:13).

Questions

- What godly purpose might your marriage fulfill in this world?
- When did you first realize your spouse was someone you would want to marry?
- How has the romance in your lives changed from when you first got together to now?

Why You Should Marry the Good Guy

*"You can date whoever you want, but you should
marry the nerds and the good guys."*
—Sheryl Sandberg

D o you have friends that seem to be in terrible relationship cycles that they should see coming like a Target Supercenter? Apparently, scientifically, some people just can't help it. While I, personally, have never been one for the whole bad-boy phenomenon, I have seen many of my best pals lay themselves across train tracks (figuratively, of course), certain that their Romeos would hit the brakes before actually dashing their hearts into a million tiny pieces. Of course, you know how that song and dance always ends: badly.

For whatever reason, many of my friends are running in the opposite direction of the "nice guy." They don't want to be gently held and told how amazing they are. They actually seem to like guys who break promises and keep them in a confusing state of noncommitment (in which these men have actually successfully fooled my friends into thinking that they are too pushy for wanting to get married after putting in a solid four years, two kids, and mortgage together) and whose attention and affection can be stolen, easily and regularly.

I used to wonder what the appeal was. Why do you want someone who actually makes you feel like you aren't good enough? I just didn't get it. And then I met Adam. Adam was the only person that, even when we were together, made me feel like we weren't. He was an excellent talker, followed up by zero action, and he would compare me to my friends on a pretty regular basis. In addition to these charming qualities, he would only call me every other day. Just in case I thought our five-hour-long phone conversation meant we were serious, he would make sure to follow up with a solid twenty-four hours of zero contact, during which I would check my phone incessantly. My friends warned me about Adam. Honestly, he wasn't even that attractive, but I was so blinded by how hard he made me work for his attention that I must have been too busy to notice.

I'm going to jump right to the end of our relationship because the fact that I have already given him a paragraph is honestly irritating. He was living in South Carolina and had driven down to spend some time with me. Before he went home, I purchased a plane ticket, as it was my turn to visit him next. I'm not sure he had even finished gassing up his car before my best friend called to tell me that he had just sent her a Myspace message. (You read that correctly—Myspace—the founding father of social networking; rest in peace). Basically, he told her he wasn't that into me and wondered if she would like to hang out sometime. I called him, enraged. He tried to deny it, and I lost a few hundred dollars on that plane ticket, but I kept regaining small fractions of my dignity every time I ignored one of his many phone calls. He continued to contact me up until he found out I was engaged to my husband before finally deleting me from his Facebook friends' list, which I think means I'm dead to him.

So why do we do this? Why do girls go all horror film and open the door for the guy that is clearly holding a machete behind his back? Well, according to research, females are much more likely than males to seek out emotionally unavailable mates. While men find nice women more attractive, women, at least in initial encounters, tend to find nice men less attractive.

One *Psychology Today* article reported that women are often attracted to "bad boys," guys who have the "Dark Triad" of toxic personality traits—narcissism, psychopathy, and Machiavellism.* Narcissistic men are not the commitment type, so if you have a closet full of Adams, you may need to ask yourself why. Could you be self-sabotaging? This is where you subconsciously seek out relationships with people you know aren't good for you. That way when it doesn't work, you can blame the lousy guy rather than your own poor choices. Sometimes we set ourselves up for failure so that when we *do* fail, we have a prop to blame.

One of my best guy friends falls in love with women who are either in relationships already or who do this on-again, off-again thing. I told him that I truly think he does this because he likes the emotional rush of being with someone, fantasizing about someone, and texting someone late at night but doesn't want the commitment of a long-term relationship. He purposefully seeks out women he knows will never commit to him and then tells these sob stories about how he is going to be thirty and single. Dude, maybe stop dating girls who are already dating other people? If a person continually seeks out relationships in which he or she knows the other person is not going to commit, it may be because this person is afraid of commitment. Cue moment of deep self-reflection.

Another reason why women may seek bad boys is if they have a real fear of victimization. Basically, if people have been victims of, let's say, sexual assault in the past, they may seek mates who have a great deal of masculine energy and who actually make them feel safer. Bad boys actually make these women feel protected, even when the bad boy is the only real risk to the woman's safety.

One last reason why many women may prefer bad boys is kind of a sad one. Narcissism runs at higher rates in men than it does women, even across cultures. If there are more bad guys out there than there are good guys, then this becomes a statistical dilemma more than a psychological one. Statistically, it is just more probable that a woman will find a narcissistic jerk to pine after than a solid, dependable man to build a life with.

* Vinita Mehta, "Why Do Women Fall for Bad Boys?" *Psychology Today*, October 21, 2013, https://www.psychologytoday.com/us/blog/head-games/201310/why-do-women-fall-bad-boys.

Can we please be mothers that birth a generation of men who don't want to hurt our daughters?

If your friends are attracted to bad boys, know that they aren't alone, but please help them end the self-sabotage. Get them off the train tracks. Tell them to stop dating Adam after Adam, expecting each time to get a different result.

I think for me, the most attractive thing about my husband is that he desperately wants to live a life that is pleasing to God. Because of this desire, he is intentional about putting our family first. He makes me dinner, leaves me notes, and tries to make me feel special because he wants to honor God, even in our marriage.

The saying goes that you should find a man whose heart is so wrapped up in God that you have to find God in order to find him. I dated an Adam once. It didn't end well.

Marrying a good guy is the best decision I ever made.

Bible Verse for Reflection

"Above all, love each other deeply, because love covers over a multitude of sins" (1 Peter 4:8).

Questions

- Did you marry the good guy? Why did you answer the way you did?
- Why should love always be kind?
- Is it realistic to think couples shouldn't argue?
- How can you handle arguments better?

When We Try to Mask Pain

Bad things do happen; how I respond to them
defines my character and the quality of my life.
I can choose to sit in perpetual sadness, immobilized by the
gravity of my loss, or I can choose to rise from the pain
and treasure the most precious gift I have—life itself.
—Walter Anderson

Pain is a loaded gun. Whether emotional or physical, introduce a high dose of pain and even the strongest, baddest, toughest among us can be immobilized. I have pushed a child out of my groin not once but *thrice*. The first time this happened I was so confused. I actually didn't understand why it felt like someone was ripping me open from the inside with a hacksaw. By the third time, I had apparently forgotten my previous two bouts with near death. I crumpled into a pile on the floor and used what was left of my depleting oxygen to mouth the word *help* to the nurse. I wanted morphine and a straw.

What if I told you that your body actually dishes out something very similar to morphine, and it's totally legal for you to use it. Hormones called *endorphins* serve one purpose in your body, and that is to mask your pain. It is your body's natural way of releasing painkillers that allows you to continue moving forward on tasks that would otherwise immobilize you.

I used to be a runner. I say "used to," because it was a past life. In fact, I am no longer even sure if it was me. I had a college scholarship for track, and at my peak, I was able to run five miles in about thirty-five minutes. Then I had children. Now I mark it a win if I pick my body up off the couch on a Sunday to snatch a Pop-Tart. That said, I do remember, once upon a time, having a good run and then getting home and taking off my shoes, only to discover my feet had blistered. Why couldn't I feel the blisters until I stopped running? Endorphins.

Endorphins don't necessarily help you feel good, but they do help you to feel less bad. And like all good drugs, you can get hooked on endorphins. This is why athletes actually *choose* to work out rather than binge-watch *Downton Abbey*. They are addicts.

In today's world, there is a *lot* to be depressed about. The United States is only in the middle of the pack in nearly every academic standard compared to their peers in many other countries. Men are ceasing to be present in fatherhood at alarming rates. Women are posting selfies and forwarding memes that quote the Dalai Lama, thinking that this somehow means they are activists for equality. Politics are contentious. A few weeks after the 2016 presidential election, a student sat in my office and talked about how emotionally painful the semester had been for her. The same was true for most of us with a newsfeed. In the midst of all the political drama, I want to offer you some good news: your body is capable of dealing with pain, and it even has a built-in defense mechanism to help you beat it.

If you are struggling through the loss of something right now, go to the gym. Exercise is one of your body's best ways of naturally masking pain. Endorphins don't just treat pain; they can also alleviate anxiety and depression. So put down the cupcake, and put on your sneakers.

Laughter is another easy way to induce a rush of endorphins. If you're married, grab your spouse and tell him you are going to go on a walk to remember the good times. Ask him to tell you a joke. It will actually allow you to breathe easier, as you will be less stifled by life's pain. Laughter, smiling, exercise—these things will help you naturally diminish your body's perception of pain, and they are a lot easier to do than stealing morphine from your local pharmacy.

The truth about pain and stress is that God wired us to need each other in order to get through these times. Stress is your body telling you that you need to reach out to someone. This is why married people live longer than single people. God knew that two are better than one when it comes to emotional health. You will survive this wait, loss, injury, and/or failure. It may take time to allow your heart to heal fully, but these tricks may help you get through the next Saturday night.

Bible Verse for Reflection
"Therefore a man shall leave his father and his mother and hold fast to his wife, and they shall become one flesh" (Genesis 2:24, ESV).

Questions
- What are you struggling with most right now?
- How can your partner best help you to carry this load?
- What is one fun thing you can do with each other today?

How to Become a Unicorn

I might act like a rhinoceros, but I'm a unicorn.
—Nuno Roque

I f you want your relationship to go to the next level of intimacy, you may have to violate it. Someone please hold my avocado; this is life-changing information.

Expectancy violations theory talks about what happens when you violate a social norm. Let's say you touch my arm while telling me a story or stand closer than you normally do while telling me how annoying your boyfriend's mother is. This is the violation of a social norm. In the United States, I don't want to smell your breath during our conversation. Back up, Jerry; let me breathe. Ironically, something interesting happens in my brain while I try to understand why you ate salsa for breakfast. According to the expectancy violations theory, I will start to produce reasoning for why you are physically so close to me. If I like the offender, my brain will create positive reasons for why a person would encroach on my personal space. Humans assume that someone is touching us because our relationship is so intimate that this type of touching is warranted.

Think about your hairdresser. Why are you telling her about that time you cheated on Brad? You haven't even told that to your own mother. Why the loose lips during a wash and rinse? Because she is standing over you, with her fingers in your hair. You aren't used to having someone run their hands through your curls, so you start to trick yourself into believing that the relationship you are currently in isn't a financial transaction. She must be your BFF; why else is this woman massaging your scalp?

When we like people and they violate us, we tend to like them *more*. Of course, if we don't like them, then the opposite is true. We end up liking the creepy guy less if he stands too close. Don't think you can waltz up to that boss who hates you and place your hand on the small of his back while asking for a raise. You'll be fired and possibly be waist deep in a harassment lawsuit. The type of violations we want only come when a genuine liking for the violator already exists.

So how does this apply to your relationship? Apparently, partners in marriages that receive only as much intimacy as they were expecting view their relationships as moderately satisfying. If your partner is unhappy, it may be that you are only *meeting* their expectation versus *exceeding* it. You are just doing the bare minimum. You are performing at the norm.

One study showed that the level of happiness in a relationship is directly tied to whether the person's expectations were met or exceeded, regardless of whether those expectations were high or low.* Their spouse held their hand *more* than they thought they needed to. They cuddled them *more* than they expected. Their brains created their own realities to explain the behaviors. They figure that if their partners do even more than they expect, they must be incredibly in love: they are my unicorn.

If you feel like your relationship is only moderately satisfying, I suggest you go above your partner's expectations in every way. Another theory, called *reciprocity*, says that human beings have a strong desire to respond to someone's actions toward us with a similar behavior. That's why you laugh at jokes that aren't that funny, just because the other person is laughing. It's why you hear yourself squeal, "Hey, girl!" at Sara even though you aren't sure if you like Sara yet. She seemed excited to see you, and so you reciprocated the intensity of her gestures. Don't think this means anything, Sara. I barely know you.

If you don't want to coast through the intimacy component of your

---

* Daisy Buchanan, "The Secret of a Happy Marriage? Low Expectations," *Guardian*, March 21, 2016, https://www.theguardian.com/commentisfree/2016/mar/21/secret-happy-marriage -low-expectations.

relationship, then don't. This is a cycle you can control. God used marriage as a symbol of our relationship with Him. That means we are supposed to serve one another, to try to outdo one another in kindness. The expectancy violations theory says you can manipulate your partner's perception of your relationship by doing more than you usually would for him or her. Rub your spouse's back without being asked. Make a sandwich for him or her. Press send on that mushy text you aren't sure is too much. Catch your spouse off guard, and it's likely he or she will feel the need to reciprocate. It will also cause your partner to view the relationship with heightened levels of love, affection, and satisfaction.

Oh, and seriously, stop telling your private biz to your hairdresser. You pay her. She probably doesn't actually *want* to rub your scalp.

Bible Verse for Reflection
"The heart of her husband trusts in her, and he will have no lack of gain. She does him good, and not harm, all the days of her life. She seeks wool and flax, and works with willing hands. She is like the ships of the merchant; she brings her food from afar. She rises while it is yet night and provides food for her household and portions for her maidens" (Proverbs 31:11–15, ESV).

Questions
- How satisfied are you in your marriage?
- Tell your partner one thing you love that he or she naturally does for you.
- Today do something delightful for your partner that he or she wasn't expecting. Wash the dishes without being asked, put away the laundry, grab some food for him or her, and so on.

I Could Taste His ChapStick

*We are afraid to care too much, for fear that
the other person does not care at all.*
—Eleanor Roosevelt

I was sixteen years old the first time I really kissed a boy. I had thought about kissing one long before that, but to be quite honest, I was terrified. I pecked a boy in the eighth grade once, and that experience was damaging enough to keep my lips sealed for four more years. He had on way too much ChapStick. I am pretty sure he slid off my face.

I didn't want to kiss him really; but after a few days of persuasion, he convinced me that when you like someone, you kiss him or her. We were "boyfriend and girlfriend," and I say that in the loosest sense of the terms, but I dumped him the day after our lips touched. I remember going home and feeling the need to shower. It was just a peck, but I felt like I had lost my virginity. In the smallest of ways, I suppose I had. Up to that point, I was completely innocent, and after a few days of persuasion, I knew what his ChapStick tasted like. I was unimpressed.

That peck left me so scarred that I dated my first high-school boyfriend for nearly six months before I kissed him. At sixteen, I had become a bit wiser to the tricks of boys; that, and my high-school boyfriend was far less pushy. When I try to think back to that first kiss in high school, I can't get a clear image. I remember it but not really. I couldn't give you any details or even transport myself back to that moment in my imagination. It wasn't memorable.

Now I *know* what a memorable kiss feels like. I've been lucky enough to have one. I was on a date with a boy whose eyes were blue. I had always thought that I preferred dark hair and dark eyes, but there I was, entranced in a river of blue, laced with long ash-colored lashes. I decided that everything I thought I knew, I didn't. He listened to every word I said. I had never felt someone listen to me so intently. The stare of those incredible eyes started to make me self-conscious. In the pit of my stomach, I wondered if he was too beautiful for me. He kept listening, so I just kept talking. I didn't think I wanted to be in another relationship so soon after my last one; but the longer he stared at me, the harder I fell.

Suddenly, he kissed me. I was in midsentence. I remember thinking that boys should ask girls for permission before they did things like that. But then I just savored the interruption. Kissing him was like drowning. I couldn't breathe. That was my last first kiss. I married the boy with the blue eyes, and with him, I have had three children with eyes equally as stunning. I can remember our first date with astounding detail. I remember the way his knuckles flexed the first time he shook the hand of my father. I can still envision that blue river breaking the first time I watched tears fall from his face. I know the smell of the sand as I lay next to him all summer. He was memorable.

I wrote a dating book in my twenties that was deeply reflective of my experience meeting my husband. It's called *Hook, Line, and Sinker*, and the whole premise is that there is a big difference between a lightning *bug* and a lightning *bolt*. Please, don't settle.

I love marriage. I still speed as I approach my neighborhood, because even though I am over seven years in, I still can't wait to be next to him. I still smell the sand. I can only say this, though, because of *who* I married, not because of marriage itself. Marriage, relationships, dating—it has to be about who you wear the label with more than the need to wear the label itself.

Remember that there is a big difference between a lightning bug and a lightning bolt. I am a woman over thirty and a mother of three who is so conservative that many of my friends lie to me about what they do on Saturday nights.

That said, there is not a day that goes by that I don't want to taste my husband's ChapStick.

Bible Verse for Reflection

"Let marriage be held in honor among all, and let the marriage bed be undefiled" (Hebrews 13:4, ESV).

Questions

- How would you describe the romantic aspect of your relationship?
- Is there anything you need your partner to give you more of, romantically?
- Describe to one another your first kiss together.

I Married My Father

*There is no more lovely, friendly, and charming relationship,
communion, or company than a good marriage.*
—Martin Luther

As a kid, I had poufy hair and braces. I was terribly skinny, and people used to joke that it looked like a bumblebee had stung my kneecaps. My family was poor, so my clothing consisted of off-brand Walmart fashions. I had a slew of secret-admirer notes wadded in my desk that had been practical jokes played on me by various girls in my classroom. I had pretty much no reason to be confident or opinionated. I should have been the shy, mousey type that fastened on my cloak of invisibility every time the bell rang. I wasn't. Despite the hundreds of reasons I had to focus my efforts on blending in, I found myself boisterously dancing around my classroom, speaking my mind to the girls at lunchtime, and unafraid to tell the cutest boy in the class to hold my hand at the roller rink. There may be several small reasons for this lunacy—a false sense of self being one of them—but the biggest contributor to my esteem was my father. He told me I was special, and I believed him.

In first grade, he sent a single rose to my classroom on Valentine's Day. All the girls whispered, wondering who it was from. I displayed it on my desk as if it was an expensive floral arrangement. When they discovered it was only from my dad, the lumps in their throats cleared. My glee didn't. He had told me I was special, and here I had a single rose on Valentine's Day to prove it.

I was eighteen years old on Valentine's Day of my senior year of high school. By then, I had tamed my poufy hair, and my braces were a distant memory. I had found boyfriends and lost them, but one thing in my life always remained consistent: my father's delivery of a single rose. It had been several years since I had prominently displayed the flower; but each time I saw it, I would smirk like I was seven years old. I had received twelve of those deliveries by that point. During my senior year of high school, I purchased a bouquet of a dozen roses and placed them on my parents' kitchen counter. It was my way of thanking my father for everything he did for me in those twelve years of good, and not so good, days that I attended school.

My father is a quiet, gentle man. He is fiercely loyal and incredibly loving. In my mind, however, I had always placed him in a box that I envisioned him staying in forever. He was my dad, and that relationship never spilled over into any other boxes. As an adult, and after nearly eleven years of studying social science, I realize that he was not *just* my dad. He became my road map to what I would look for in a husband.

According to Elayne Savage, a psychotherapist based out of Berkeley, California, one of the biggest reasons we choose our partners is because of familiarity. She says, "When you grow up familiar with a certain type of person, you're attracted to that same type of person because it feels comfortable, whether you like it or not. . . . That's what people mean when they meet a potential partner and say, 'It feels like I've known him my whole life.' "*

I met my husband in the sixth grade. I was eleven years old, and while I did form a bond with him in those years, his family moved an hour away two years later. I didn't speak to him again until I was twenty-two, but what struck me the most on our first date was that I had never felt so comfortable with someone. I understood him. We would stay up at night talking for hours, and every time he displayed passion for God or having

* Celeste Perron, "Why You're Likely to Marry Your Parent," CNN, February 11, 2009, http://www.cnn.com/2009/LIVING/personal/02/11/lw.programmed.to.marry.parents/.

a dream, I fell harder in love. At the time, I truly believed I had met the most unique man with the most gentle and loyal heart; but now, looking back, I realize those are the same words I would use to describe my dad.

It's not just women who do this either. A researcher out of the University of Iowa analyzed thirty-seven hundred high-achieving men. She found that men in the top 10 percent of their income bracket and/or with a graduate degree had an overwhelming propensity to seek out partners that mirrored their mothers in both education and career achievement.*

My experience with my father was a blessed one. Our bond is of spiritual proportions, and I am so grateful to have followed that pattern while choosing my husband. That said, many of us don't have childhood memories of roses. My husband, for example, loves his father but has been deeply impacted by many years where he was, quite frankly, absent. According to research, many of us will subconsciously seek out mates who resemble our parents in an attempt to change the narrative. Sometimes women who felt abandoned by their fathers continually seek out relationships with men who are emotionally unavailable. It is the psyche's way of going back to painful memories and undoing them.† Unfortunately, we are often no more equipped to deal with those unhappy memories now than we were at seven, and the parental dynamic that hindered our childhood puts us in a path of repetition.

Here's what I know: my daughter is one of the most independent, confident little girls I have ever met. She genuinely thinks she should contribute her point of view to every adult conversation. She is feisty and strong, and while I would like to take all the credit for that, I know that a lot of it comes from her father. He's woven into her perception of self every time he takes her on a "date." It has shaped her esteem every time she sings a song, and my husband races for his phone to record it. She thinks she is pretty special, and while I know I am also pivotal to her self-concept, I am so grateful that I married a man who can give her

---

* "Study: It Might Be True That 'Men Marry Their Mothers,'" University of Iowa News Services, May 5, 2008, http://news-releases.uiowa.edu/2008/may/050508marry_mothers.html.

† Perron, "Why You're Likely to Marry Your Parent."

the affirmation that I know I needed as a child.

That said, some of us have chains to break, and if you are terrified of repeating your past, please know that those relationships do not have to define you as long as you are conscious about the patterns they may have created.

So yes, somehow I unintentionally married my father. I hope every man understands how crucial his parental role is not only in his child's past and present but also in his child's future.

Bible Verse for Reflection
"With all humility and gentleness, with patience, bearing with one another in love, eager to maintain the unity of the Spirit in the bond of peace" (Ephesians 4:2, 3, ESV).

Questions
- Does your spouse have similarities to either of your parents?
- Which of your spouse's traits do you hope to see in your child?
- What childhood experiences do you think lead you to want a spouse like the one you have?

The Other Woman

When people show you who they are, believe them the first time.
—Oprah Winfrey

You have lost count of the lies. The number of times he has held you in his arms and told you that you are the only woman who truly knows him. His eyes are convincing, but you know better. You've seen it. The way he jumps for her. The lengths he would go to make sure she is taken care of. She knows it too. It's this unspoken, awkward dance the two of you play around him. Both of you laughing at his jokes, trying to outdo one another with enthusiasm. He loves her, and a part of you worries that if he had to choose between the two of you, he may hesitate. But then you feel crazy, foolish, even disgusted with yourself because she is his mother.

I got a text from a friend a few weeks ago. She had a question about her mother-in-law. She said she couldn't think of anyone who had a good relationship with their partner's mother and then she thought of me. It's true. I have a fantastic bond with my mother-in-law. I even call her mom. She has been a blessing to me and was a safe place to vent in the beginning of my marriage when I struggled with both loving and hating my husband at the same time. I thought I was marrying a perfect man, and it turns out I didn't. I didn't know who I could confide in with this shocking news, so I went to her. She loved him as much as I did, so I knew I could trust her to keep loving him despite whatever I needed to say. I love my mother-in-law, which is why I think it is safe for me to write this. I want to say what many women need to hear but are too afraid, embarrassed, or stubborn to admit. Your husband loves another woman, and sometimes it makes you jealous.

This isn't new. Many women don't even like their mothers-in-law. Basically, before social media forced you to play nice, a deep-seated tension had already been planted. Dr. Terri Apter, a psychologist at Cambridge University, studied hundreds of families and found that nearly two-thirds of women claim to have suffered long-term unhappiness because their mothers-in-law created stress and friction. While wives said that their husbands' moms were trying to create friction in their marriage, the mothers said that their sons' wives were trying to exclude them from their sons' lives.*

Dr. Apter studied this phenomenon for more than two decades. She found that the reason for the strife is that both women seek to be the primary woman or mother in the household because the households overlap. She found that while wives feel that their mothers-in-law are constantly judging their parenting, cleaning, and cooking skills, mothers-in-law often feel that the daughters-in-law are rejecting their wisdom and advice. One Italian study found that the odds your marriage will last increase with every hundred yards that a couple puts between themselves and their in-laws.†

Dr. Apter interviewed more than two hundred families and found that 75 percent had issues with in-laws. Only 15 percent of those were problems between the husband and his in-laws. One reason for this may be that men tend to react differently than women when it comes to conflict. In communications research, we teach that men tend to be conflict *thinkers*, while women tend to be conflict *feelers*. If you have a minute, check the Mother-In-Law Stories website (http://www.motherinlawstories.com) and see just

---

* Murray Wardrop, "Wives Find Mothers in Law Hardest to Deal With," *Telegraph*, November 30, 2008, https://www.telegraph.co.uk/news/uknews/3536796/Wives-find-mothers-in-law-hardest-to-deal-with.html.

† Terry Apter, " 'She Made Me Feel Quite Inadequate as a Mother,' " *Daily Mail*, September 21, 2017, https://www.dailymail.co.uk/femail/article-4904130/nothing-s-maddening-meddling-mother-law.html.

how intense the battle of the primary woman can become. It's brutal.

The truth is that in many cases, your husband picked you because you reminded him of her. Many studies have found that people tend to look for mates who have traits reminiscent of those they saw in their opposite-gender parent.* In a normal, nontoxic family environment, men learn to love from their moms, so when they seek mates, they knowingly or unknowingly reference that love.

At best, recognize that you and your mother-in-law likely have a lot in common. You both fiercely love the same man and want what's best for him. You probably also have more than that in common. At worst, respect the fact that she is his mother.

I have two sons. Right now, if you asked Hudson who he is going to marry, he would smile and say, "Mommy." That's not true. One day he will meet a girl, and his loyalty to me will sever. I hope when that day comes, I will be mentally prepared for him to move past my arms and into someone else's. It is with optimism that I tell myself that the woman he chooses to take my place won't freeze me out. That little boy melts my heart. And while she may love him then, I loved him *first*.

As you vent about your mother-in-law, remember that she may be "the other woman," but one day most of us will be too.

Bible Verse for Reflection

"And over all these virtues put on love, which binds them all together in perfect unity" (Colossians 3:14).

Questions
- What is your relationship like with your in-laws?
- How could your spouse help make that relationship better?
- What is one experience where you felt like you really got along with your in-laws?

---

* Peg Streep, "Why Your Partner May Be Like Your Parent," *Psychology Today*, May 13, 2014, https://www.psychologytoday.com/us/blog/tech-support/201405/why-your-partner-may-be-your-parent.

There Is More to Life Than Him

There is always some madness in love, but there is always some reason in madness.
—Friedrich Nietzsche

I always loved books. I can remember, as a child, walking into my school library and feeling intoxicated by the smell of the books encasing the room. I liked the weight of a novel in my hands and the feeling of pages flipping past my fingers. As a child when I dreamed about my life, my dreams were always about writing books. That is all I wanted.

By middle school, I wanted boys. I wanted them to want me too. I wrote in journals about the various boys that I liked and had a shoebox beneath my bed with all the notes I received. I still loved books but not more than I loved receiving those notes. If you had asked me at the age of twelve what my dreams were, I would still have told you that I dreamed of writing books, but that wasn't the complete truth. When you want something badly, you focus your energy on it. You spend your free time trying to propel yourself to reach goals. I spent my energy learning how to apply eye shadow, and I saved all my allowance to buy denim that made my butt look good. My other dreams had faded, and I was always shotgun in someone's truck.

I like to think that I was driven; but in truth, I think I was oftentimes distracted. I was the girl who always had a boyfriend. I didn't have a string of boys that I ran through but long-term relationships. I am embarrassed to admit this, but my entire life from the time I turned fourteen until I was twenty-two can be chronicled by a series of three boyfriends. Want to know how I decided which college I was going to? I tell people it was because I got a track scholarship, but the truth is that I only applied to one school—the one my boyfriend was attending. My mother warned me not to choose my education based on a romance, but she didn't understand— I loved him.

We broke up before the fall semester had even ended. For the first time since I was fourteen years old, I was single, and to be honest, I didn't quite know who I was. I transferred schools at the end of the year, and I decided that I was going to find myself. That lasted a few months, and before I knew it, I was dating again and then engaged. I remember telling my ex-fiancé that I wanted to be a professor, and he told me that going to school that many years would take too long and he wanted to have a family. We broke up two months before our wedding. That same summer I got my very first publishing contract. I felt like I was dying inside, and yet here I received this email saying that my childhood dreams were going to come true. I could write books. I could allow my fingers to feel the strum of pages I had written. I took it as a sign from the universe that there was more to life than him.

I have a husband. I love him dearly. He is honestly my soul mate, and I am pretty sure God chose him to partner through life with me. That said, my husband doesn't make me who I am. He *betters* me, but he doesn't *make* me. I have come to a place in my life where I believe that there has to be more to life than him. It takes a romantic, caring woman to live life for someone else. It takes a driven, secure, confident woman to live life for herself.

Remember what your dreams are, and chase after them for you. You are God's only shot at you. When He made you, He built you with the ability to grab a hold of whatever is rooted deep inside of you and to change the world with it. You are not just a person; you are a plan. It's a wonderful thing to find love. But it is a life-giving thing to find purpose.

Whether you are married or single, a mother or a daughter, I hope you don't ever lose what it is about you that makes you different from everyone else. You are not just a person; you are a plan. Let your partner make you better, but don't let them make you, you. There is more to life than him.

Bible Verse for Reflection

"For husbands, this means love your wives, just as Christ loved the church. He gave up his life for her" (Ephesians 5:25, NLT).

Questions

- Do you feel like you have an identity outside of your relationship?
- Is there something you always wanted to do before you got married or were in a serious relationship that you have since stopped thinking about?
- How has marriage helped you make new dreams?

What I Wanted in a Man

My most brilliant achievement was my ability
to persuade my wife to marry me.
—Winston Churchill

When I was fifteen, my friends and I made dating contracts. It was a list of all the qualities potential boyfriends would need to have in order to make the cut. We signed them in blood and pinky swore we would never settle for a boy who did not check off our requirements.

Sometimes I listen to my single friends, and I hear similar lists tossed around. He has to make good money, and he has to want three kids. He better be fine or else what exactly have I been waiting for? I can't help but notice, as a woman who is quite a few years deep into my actual legally binding relationship contract, that, in some ways, the man I now call husband may not have checked all the boxes on my list.

At the age of fifteen, I couldn't have known what I wanted in a man or in the father of my children. If I were to create a list at twenty-five, I still wouldn't have been able to itemize some of the qualities he has that I never knew I wanted. Some things in life you can't know until you experience them.

For fun, my husband looks at paint swatches. He often comes home radiating with the glow of a man who has recently spent time at a Lowe's. He has no idea what Pinterest is, but the guy could build you a lakefront cabin out of shoelaces and bubble gum. How was I to know that I would fall madly in love with a man who thinks that an acceptable outing for a date is going to a bait-and-tackle shop? I didn't choose this life, y'all; it chose me.

Late at night he will nudge my shoulder. He is testing to see if I'm asleep. I know what he is thinking. Sometimes I pretend I am already crashed, because I am simply not in the mood. Other nights I provide proof of life, and he shyly asks if I want to go get a snack. (Not what you were thinking, right? Stay out of grown folks' business.) We tiptoe down the stairs so that we don't wake any monster children. When he is talking dirty, he'll ask if I want any dairy. The struggling vegan inside of me quivers.

I've come home early from work to find that he invited our elderly neighbor over to watch the news. My husband doesn't watch the news. He just pretends he's concerned with the direction of the Dow to give Max something to gripe about and a pair of ears who will listen. I wouldn't have put that in my boyfriend contracts. But it has made me more sympathetic to his dirty socks on my bedroom floor.

I married a man who won't just pull over if you are stranded on the side of the road with a flat tire; he'll put your towing bill on his credit card and refuse to give you his name. One time he said we had to make a quick stop on our way to dinner. I had three kids in the car, but he swore it would only take a second. Next thing I know, we are entering a Shady Acres Mobile Home Park. Before I can object, he is out the door, and a man named Bob is heading toward him on a scooter. He talks to him for a moment, and then they pray. He hands Bob a new tackle box with several lures and gets back into the car as if this was just another Tuesday. As we drove out of the trailer park, I felt overwhelmed with pride that this was the man I married. There was no box to check for that on the potential-husband-qualifications list.

Tell all your single friends to throw out the lists. They can free themselves of the boxes that need checking. Most of the women I know who are happily married have husbands that don't check the boxes they thought they wanted, yet have qualities they never imagined they'd need.

The thing about life is that if you plan it too closely, you won't ever get lost in the moments you are living in. Go on the date with the shy guy that has profile pictures from that Star Wars convention. You can't fit hearts into boxes, and if you try, you could miss out on a man whose laugh is so contagious you forget you are in the aisles of a Costco.

And to my married friends, don't forget, every now and then, to step into his world. Pretend you are scintillated by his paint swatches. Put *Star Wars* on, and laugh at the impersonations he does that inside make you cringe. Let him feel like he is the guy of your dreams, even if he wasn't. You didn't know what you wanted until you found what you needed.

I thought I knew what I wanted in a man, but I indexed all the wrong things. Burn your list.

Bible Verse for Reflection

"Two are better than one, because they have a good return for their labor: If either of them falls down, one can help the other up. But pity anyone who falls and has no one to help them up. Also, if two lie down together, they will keep warm. But how can one keep warm alone?" (Ecclesiastes 4:9–11).

Questions

- What was on your list?
- What is something about your partner's personality you now know you need but never thought of before?
- Make a list of five qualities your spouse has that you didn't realize you wanted.

I Stopped Laughing at His Jokes

An hour of play reveals more than a year of conversation.
—H. Addington Bruce

When I was twenty-two, my now-husband was the funniest man on Earth. My cheeks hurt every time I was with him. We would have dance parties on the living-room floor and talk into the wee hours of the morning, and I'd giggle like he was a professional comedian and I had a backstage pass. I am not sure when exactly his jokes stopped being prime-time comedy, but at some point between dirty laundry and a pile of dishes, my husband's jokes got less funny.

My sister-in-law was in town visiting recently. Every joke my husband tossed she caught with enthusiasm. He looked alive. His eyes were wide, and his mouth was in a permanent grin. For hours, I watched him take out the old comedy routine I had put out of business. He was back on stage, and people were buying tickets. As I took in the scene, I realized two things: (1) my husband is actually funny, and (2) I am a total wench.

Why do we do this? I can't be the only woman in the world to sprain my neck from how hard I roll my eyes in my husband's direction. I am supposed to be his biggest fan, and here I had pulled the plug on his tour. Suddenly, as I watched my husband come alive under the appreciation of another woman (Thank You, Jesus, it was only his sister), I realized that this is probably how men end up tempted to cheat. People don't set out to have affairs. These things often happen gradually, and I would assume that the first step is as simple as someone making him feel special, interesting, and desirable.

By the way, if I told a joke and my husband didn't laugh, I would be mad. Are you deaf, dude? I am so funny. Laugh like you mean it.

Studies show that men are more likely to view their wives and their relationships as perfect.* Women, on the other hand, use many words to describe their partners, and "perfect" is rarely one of them. I think these trends are actually passed down to us from childhood. In a healthy family home, little boys grow up being told by Dad that their mothers are beautiful, graceful, and perfect. Little girls grow up watching Mother roll her eyes every time Dad hits the punch line. And when boys try to describe their mothers, they use similar language as their fathers used.

When you ask little girls about Dad, they say that he is great and loving, but he always gets the wrong items at the grocery store. Mommy makes sure we know how many faults he has. Dad doesn't wipe the counters down, he leaves the toilet seat up, and he watches dumb television shows—the list goes on. Girls learn early that dads are lovable but never perfect. I guarantee if you were to ask my children right now if Mom is perfect, they would say yes without missing a beat. I don't credit that to me; I credit that to the way they see their father treat me. I am the queen, and he is the goon. Except he's not, and I must make sure they know that.

Today I am going to remind myself to make my husband feel like a man. I am going to try to see him through my twenty-two-year-old eyes. I am going to acknowledge everything he does right rather than pinpoint the one thing he did wrong. And I am going to laugh at his jokes. I'm going to buy a front-row ticket and let him pull out the old routine.

Your husband is funny. Don't forget to notice.

Bible Verse for Reflection

"Dear friends, let us love one another, for love comes from God. Everyone

---

* Susan Sprecher and Sandra Metts, "Development of the 'Romantic Beliefs Scale' and Examination of the Effects of Gender and Gender-Role Orientation," *Journal of Social and Personal Relationships* 16, no. 6 (November 1989): 387–411, https://doi.org/10.1177/0265407589064001.

who loves has been born of God and knows God. Whoever does not love does not know God, because God is love" (1 John 4:7, 8).

Questions

- What is something you love about your spouse's sense of humor?
- Have you found you no longer laugh at each other's jokes? Why?
- Pay attention to each other today. Be each other's fans.

I Stopped Sleeping With My Husband

The strength of a man and wife joined together in God's sight is far
greater than the sum of the strengths of each of the two individuals.
—Stormie Omartian

This has been a tough year for me. We added a third child into our family. I am finishing my dissertation, and I have felt like I am running myself ragged at work. Not to mention that it seems as if everyone in my family has contracted the bubonic plague this year. I'm popping Advil Cold & Sinus like it's a street drug, and I considered showing up at my family doctor with a firearm, demanding a magic potion to give me my energy back. Life has been hectic, and every relationship right now feels strained. A few years ago my husband and I started doing something that has deeply impacted our marriage for the better.

We stopped sleeping together.

Equilibrium theory says that intimacy and distance vary together. I know that this is true every time my husband continues watching an episode of *Alaskan Bush People* even after I have told him to stop. If I hear one more clan member refer to "Browntown," I will set the television on fire. I "burn" holes through the side of his face with my eyes, all while sitting as far from him on the couch as possible. My brain cells start dwindling the second Bear and Snowbird ask Pa for a lick of the family lolly. (If you've no idea what I'm talking about here, consider yourself blessed.) My husband and I tend to sit close to one another in the evening but not during *Alaskan Bush People*. I'm seething. And equilibrium theory says that the level of intimacy I feel will correlate to the level of distance I keep between us on that couch.

There are some days that we are virtual ships in the night. I barely see him. In between running to and from work and errands today, I stopped by my house. My husband was standing in the driveway when I pulled in, and at the sight of me, he smiled. There was something really warm about the way his face lit up. After seven years of marriage and three kids, he still blushes when he sees me. It felt like high school. I had to teach a night class, so I didn't stay long. But for the rest of the evening, my mind wandered back to that effortless grin he gave me. I needed that moment with him in a day that would be largely marked by his absence.

Despite our terrible schedules this year, illness, and *Alaskan Bush People*, my husband and I made a choice a few years ago that I think keeps us intimately connected, and I think you should try it. *We stopped sleeping together.*

At five o'clock every morning, we stop sleeping. We get up in the dark, fumble our way down the stairs, and make coffee. Before we run off to our separate locations for the day and alternating commitments we have made, we have worship together. It's our time to sit—uninterrupted—with no kids, no social media, and no television. It's just the two of us, facing one another on the couch, bonding. I look forward to each morning as if it's a romantic date, only it's our living room sofa, and my teeth aren't brushed.

I can see how many couples suffer from affairs. Life gets busy. We spend more time at work than we do at home. So at 5:00 A.M., before the sun is up, my husband and I make sure to close the distance. We stop sleeping.

At first it was hard, but now it feels easy. I can't imagine going to work without first having sat across from him. When I am on my deathbed, one of the memories from my life that will sit like fog in my mind is watching my husband read his Bible in a giant plush robe on our couch. And I just want to throw this out there: there are few things in life more intimate than kneeling beside someone in prayer. When I go to work after worship with him, his heart comes with me.

About three years ago, I stopped sleeping with my husband. We get up while the world is still dark and my kids are still quiet. Life is busy. The day won't just give you time for your relationship. You are going to have to make it.

Bible Verse for Reflection

"Let them give thanks to the LORD for his unfailing love and his wonderful deeds for mankind, for he satisfies the thirsty and fills the hungry with good things" (Psalm 107:8, 9).

Questions

- Do you think you and your partner spend enough alone time together?
- When was the last time you planned a date?
- Try setting your alarm an hour early tomorrow and commit to spending that time together.

My Lesbian Neighbors

*"Chains do not hold a marriage together. . . . It is threads, hundreds
of tiny threads which sew people together through the years."*
—Simone Signoret

I live in a nice upper-class community. The type of place where you can
go for long walks and wave to Randy while he throws rib eyes on the
barbie.

A lesbian couple lives in the neighborhood. At least, I assume they are
lesbians. They could, of course, be BFFs who prefer crew cuts. I've never
asked. It seems inappropriate to question people's sexual orientation on
afternoon strolls. Nonetheless, I make it a point to always smile when
I drive by their house and they are in the yard. I wave or nod my head.
Mind you, I run like Usain Bolt from all my heterosexual neighbors'
chitchat, but I smile and wave like Mr. Rogers when I pass my two lady
friends. I didn't even recognize I was doing this until this summer, and we
have lived here two years. I guess subconsciously I wanted to make sure
my neighbors felt welcomed by me. I didn't know if they had experienced
any long stares or rude comments from people at work, so I wanted to
make sure they felt welcomed at home.

Christ said to love your neighbors as yourself, and then this lawyer
interrogated Him: "And who is my neighbor?" (Luke 10:29). He says this
in an attempt to pin Christ down. The religious folk are seriously riled up
that this Guy claiming to be the Messiah keeps throwing passive digs at
their establishment. Christ enters the synagogue and says that the rabbis

have turned a house of God into a den of robbers.

Today that may look like Jesus showing up at a supertrendy worship service and asking why there's a coffee shop and pyrotechnics in the sanctuary. Or popping into an ultraconservative, right-wing praise session to take over the podium and talk about wolves in sheep's clothing. The church doesn't often remind us that it wasn't the Romans or secular society that were screaming "Crucify Him!" It was the religious folk. The church was ultimately responsible for rejecting the One who came to save them. They thought Christ was obnoxious because He kept overthrowing their hierarchy. They didn't think a radical like Jesus could ever truly be the Messiah.

In my case, the lesbian couple are my literal neighbors, but I believe in treating people kindly regardless of where they receive their Amazon Prime deliveries. It's funny because in Luke chapter 10, a lawyer asks Jesus who our neighbors are, and Christ responds by telling the story of the good Samaritan. Jesus did this a lot. Rather than directly tell people they were wrong, He would tell them stories until they were able to answer their own questions. It was like *The Wonder Years* sitcom with those deep, self-reflecting narration moments that had you rethinking all your awful choices: I want to be a better person because Kevin Arnold is a stand-up guy.

Christ tells the lawyer, and the crowd that is listening to their interaction, about the holy man and priest that walk right by a man who has been robbed and beaten and left for dead. They can't tell if he is a neighbor, which in their case meant another Jew, or if he is a Gentile, which meant he wasn't one of them. He is beaten so badly it's hard to tell whether he is a member of the in group or the out group, so they look the other way and pass by him. The holy guys pass a dying man in need of help because they have tricked themselves into believing that help belongs to the "righteous." The Samaritan (an outsider and enemy nation of the Jews) stops and helps the man and puts him on his own donkey and pays for his food and lodging until he is better. The "unrighteous" nation performs the act of mercy that the righteous men refused to do because they only loved their neighbors.

Christ asks the lawyer which man acted justly, and the man, who can't even stomach saying the word *Samaritan*, says instead, "The one who had mercy on him" (Luke 10:37).

I've seen a lot of memes swirling around Facebook lately. Some make fun of people by race, socioeconomic ranking, religious affiliation, or most often, various political positions. The other day I cackled with my best friend about an obnoxious post someone made, and later that night I couldn't sleep.

"Who is your neighbor?" I felt God whisper. Is it just people who think like me, talk like me, and vote like me? Or is it also that obnoxious internet troll that keeps shouting with a series of exclamation marks? How do I genuinely love people I disagree with? Funny thing is, I do it all the time; it's just that I call them *family*. But that's the thing; the human race is just one giant family, so we *can* love each other without endorsing each other's point of view.

I need to do better. You catch more bees with honey than vinegar. The best thing to break darkness is light. If I can't stand someone's ignorance, I should be more poignant with my truth. If I can't stomach someone's hate, I should be more open with how I love. And if I don't like your politics, I should stop and think about what qualities of yours I do admire. I can't just appreciate people who think like me. That's too easy. I have to learn to love people who don't give me much to love. The best way to actually become a Christian is to act like one.

So today, when you pull in to your neighborhood, make sure to smile and wave to your lesbian neighbors. I'm going to work up the courage to chat with my heterosexual ones too—but in my own time, people. Don't rush me.

Bible Verse for Reflection

"As for you, my friends, you were called to be free. But do not let this freedom become an excuse for letting your physical desires control you. Instead, let love make you serve one another. For the whole Law is summed up in one commandment: 'Love your neighbor as you love yourself' " (Galatians 5:13, 14, GNT).

Questions

- Who is your enemy?
- How can you give this person or these people to God?
- Do your actions reveal a Christian heart towards God's people? Why or why not?

I Am Tired of Being Happy

Happy is he who finds a true friend. Happier still is he
who finds in his own wife a true friend.
—Franz Schubert

I f you opened this book today looking for a pick-me-up, exit immediately. I got nothing for you. A student once stayed after my class to ask what my zodiac sign was. She said, "I just love that you are always so happy." I immediately flinched and waited to see if Zeus would strike me with a bolt of lightning. (Kidding, of course.) I had been a lot of things during that time, but happy isn't one of them.

Is it just me, or does it feel like the world is dark? When I say "the world is dark," I actually mean people. I am tired of a lot of things lately, and one of which is passing the buck. "The world" being dark is a vague and cliché way of me actually saying people are mean and rude, and I am tired of it.

I'm tired of watching one of my best friends drag herself from place to place, begging people to donate fifty dollars, thirty dollars, or even give her an IOU for five bucks, and she would scream, "Bless you!" All this peddling is so she can answer the burden she's been carrying to build a school so kids in Zimbabwe can learn. Do you know how many churches you have to visit in order to find someone who's more action than apathy? James 2:15, 16 reads like a clapback tweet these days: "Suppose a brother or a sister is without clothes and daily food. If one of you says to them, 'Go in peace; keep warm and well fed,' but does nothing about their physical needs, what good is it?"

People act like she is asking them to grab a shovel. You don't actually have to roll up your sleeves and *do* anything. She'll do all the work. Could you just forego one pair of LuLaRoe leggings so that she can dig a well and get these kids clean water? #blessings.

I am tired of listening to my single friends go on bad date after bad date with guys who seem nice when offering to pull out their chairs but are impatient when they won't pull off their pants.

I am tired of politics. I am tired of defining myself by a political party that doesn't care about me. I am sick of companies stamping pink ribbons on their products and donating as much of their profits to actual breast cancer treatment as my kids have in their piggy banks. People are actually *making money* off cancer! If that doesn't make you want to shred your clothing and wail in the streets, I don't think I can be friends with you.

While we are here, now is as good a time as any to tell you how much I hate porn. An alarming percentage of college-age males admit that they would rape a woman if no one would find out.* Of course, they don't actually say the *R* word, but when you ask them if it is acceptable to have sex with a girl who passes out in the middle of a make-out sesh, they don't see why not.

I wore my "Porn kills love" T-shirt the other day, and a student asked me why I didn't like porn. (If you are actually interested in some of the issues related to porn, search YouTube for a TED Talk by Gary Wilson called "The Great Porn Experiment." He's a little nerdy, but the research is killer.) Look, I don't have the energy to break down a dissertation on neuroscience here, but we are fooling ourselves if we actually think that what we are watching isn't shaping our brains. ("Reality" television, I'm looking at you too.) I personally believe chivalry died when porn was born. I don't care if you don't agree with me. No need to tweet me or press send on that impressive email you are crafting. Go ahead and keep up the

---

* Victoria Bekiempis, "When Campus Rapists Don't Think They're Rapists," *Newsweek*, January 9, 2015, https://www.newsweek.com/campus-rapists-and-semantics-297463.

valiant and heroic fight of justifying an industry that capitalizes off of the exploitation of women and children. Good luck with that.

I am sick of beautiful, intelligent, hilarious women struggling to patch bullet holes with duct tape. More than one out of four children in this country are robbed of feeling loved by the dad who created them. This one relationship failure makes kids four times more likely to live in poverty, seven times more likely to experience teenage pregnancy, and twice as likely to drop out of high school.* Let's give a round of applause to the men who are actually being men. If you aren't calling out your deadbeat son, brother, or boyfriend for the way he treats the kids he fathered, then you are part of the problem.

Also, can we make a unanimous decision right now to stop ghosting people? If you want to break up with someone, have a face-to-face conversation with him or her. Don't just stop answering calls or change your status on social media. These are real people, not game pieces. If you want to end a relationship, a friendship, or a business partnership, have a conversation. It will absolutely be uncomfortable, but it is imperative to give people closure. Ghosting out may be convenient, but it is also cowardly and dehumanizing. We strip away at people's dignity and then wonder why people are so depressed. Of course we are!

I'm seriously tired of encouraging people to "cheer up" because "it'll get better." They're emotionally cold and soaking wet, and I am supposed to pretend I don't notice? I don't have the right answer for you. I don't want to point to a bright side because sometimes there isn't one. Sometimes it just feels awful, and I think it is more beneficial for me to say that and to give you permission to feel whatever it is you feel right now. It is OK not to be happy. You don't have to fake it.

There is *a lot* of darkness in this world, and I don't want to shift the blame anymore. This is us. We are doing this to each other. We are divided and selfish and cruel. This is who we are, myself included.

---

* "The Father Absence Crisis in America," National Fatherhood Initiative, infographic, accessed September 19, 2018, https://www.fatherhood.org/fatherhood-data-statistics.

So no, things aren't fine, and I am tired of being happy. Today I'm just going to be real, and I hope you will forgive me for failing.

Bible Verse for Reflection
"Your love, LORD, reaches to the heavens, your faithfulness to the skies. Your righteousness is like the highest mountains, your justice like the great deep" (Psalm 36:5, 6).

Questions
- What are you struggling to be happy about?
- What burdens do you need to ask God to carry today?
- What can your partner do to be a bright spot for you today? Tell him or her.

Seven Things a Mom Did Before She Even Got to Work

*"That's who my mom is. She's a listener and a doer.
She's a woman driven by compassion, by faith,
by a fierce sense of justice, and a heart full of love."*
—Chelsea Clinton

I t's 10:48 A.M., and I have just arrived at my place of employment. Everyone's all "Good morning!" and I'm just doing my best to blend in. I literally noticed snot on the front of my dress while I was backing out of my driveway this morning. I had to run back in for a quick wardrobe change after already carefully selecting my attire three hours ago.

This is the life of a working mom: thinking you have your stuff together one moment and then making a mad dash into the house as you realize you ain't got nothin'.

Here are seven things we working moms probably do before we even get to work:

1. You have probably had your fingers up somebody's nose. Now just pause with me. When you pictured your life ten years ago, is this what you imagined for yourself?

2. You have made everybody, except yourself, breakfast. I'm not pretending anything extravagant has gone on. But at least in my situation, for three different people, sometimes four if my husband is lucky, I have cracked open a box of frozen waffles, spread butter not once but thrice,

90

and turned my kitchen into a school cafeteria assembly line. I can cut apple slices in my sleep and make peanut-butter toast better than Gordon Ramsay. Ask me what I ate for breakfast, and nine out of ten times, you are going to hear me say, "Coffee." After you prepare food for three other people, you forget that you also need to eat something. You grab a cookie out of the pantry and shout "No!" before your kids even ask if they can have one too.

3. You have yelled. You don't want to be this person. No one wants to be the mean mom that is always raising her voice and tickling the curiosity of her neighbors. But it's 7:45 A.M., and you have five minutes to get three small bodies into car seats, with shoes and socks on. By the way, as you're backing out of the driveway, you learn that it's show-and-tell day, and if your son doesn't have something to show and tell about, you will have singlehandedly destroyed his entire life. The time for niceties passed when little Jimmy thought it would be a good idea to take out your mixing bowls and create a hot tub for his action figures. Right now, it's go time, and that means your children either fall in line or you receive one of those lovely letters from the principal, alerting you to how many tardies your child has had that school season. You aren't a deadbeat, for crying out loud, so you yell, "Get your shoes and get in the car!" loud enough to cut through their chatter and also the sleepy eyes of your neighborhood.

4. You have cried. Look, I try to be a Christian woman. I wake up at 5:00 A.M. to drink coffee and meditate on the scriptural wisdoms of Jesus Christ. But something happens when you have two kids fighting over who sits in the middle seat and a baby who thinks it's in his job description to destock the items from your pantry and let Cheez-Its rain on your kitchen floor. You snap. You raise your voice. You threaten to shred that precious blue cereal bowl in the trash compactor after the 350th straight morning of hearing high-pitched voices argue over who got to use it last. I'm a Christian, not a saint. Before I've even read your passive-aggressive email that begins with: "As previously stated," I've already lost it at least once and then felt bad about it. I may or may not have already cried before I even showed up at work today. Have mercy on me.

5. You've probably delivered a motivational speech. I'm not comparing myself to Martin Luther King Jr. or anything, but I *do* my fair share of Denzel Washington meets Meryl Streep three to five days a week. Every now and then, I'll open my mouth and wisdom just falls out of it. I'm mediating fights, reminding people to respect themselves and others, and doling out self-esteem sound bites while driving down US 31. I've got more inspirational material than a Chinese fortune-cookie factory. *I'm making America great again.*

6. You've been barged in on. My kids and I have this fun game we play where I get in the shower or go to the restroom, and then they decide that this is actually the optimum time to tell me about the leaf that blew into the street yesterday. That's the whole story. That is what simply couldn't wait. There was this leaf, and it blew into the street. The end.

7. You took a deep breath. Maybe you did it in the car after the kids were gone. Maybe it was right before you placed your hand on the door that would lead you to the rooms filled with adult people and adult conversation. Or maybe it was when you sat down at your desk and realized you had fifty-plus emails to respond to. Either way, at some point, you took a deep breath and tried to transition your headspace from at-home mom to workplace mom. That deep breath allows you to put on a smile and try to look normal.

Some days you get to work already feeling accomplished, and other days you show up already feeling crushed. While everyone else puts themselves first, you have no choice but to put yourself last. You are truly a walking inspiration. But there will be no accolades nor praise for everything you did this morning. Your work goes silent and largely unnoticed because it is so deeply ingrained in the fabric of who you are. You aren't just a working mom. You are also a forgotten hero.

Don't forget to take the deep breath. God often speaks in silence. You'll need it.

Bible Verse for Reflection

"Strength and dignity are her clothing, and she laughs at the time to come.

She opens her mouth with wisdom, and the teaching of kindness is on her tongue. She looks well to the ways of her household and does not eat the bread of idleness. Her children rise up and call her blessed; her husband also, and he praises her: 'Many women have done excellently, but you surpass them all' " (Proverbs 31:25–30, ESV).

Questions

- How hard is the balance right now of mommy and wife and worker?
- Do you feel like God sees how hard you are trying? How so?
- Today don't do it all. Ask your partner for help.

One Day My Kid Will Be in High School

Motherhood is a great honor and privilege, yet it is also synonymous with servanthood. Every day women are called upon to selflessly meet the needs of their families. Whether they are awake at night nursing a baby, spending their time and money on less-than-grateful teenagers, or preparing meals, moms continuously put others before themselves.
—Charles Stanley

This year my daughter will start first grade, which means I am naturally already having crippling anxiety over her first day of high school. My friend, *What was high school?*

I went to the principal's office once. I asked him to repaint the bathroom stalls. People had written my name next to the word *slut*, and I didn't appreciate the correlation, even if it was in cursive. I didn't kiss a boy until I was sixteen years old. But that didn't matter in high school. Because what you *actually* did or didn't do never mattered as much as the stories people told. Thank goodness there wasn't a Facebook in 2003. None of us would pass any HR background check.

Surviving high school was like being tossed into some high-pressure social experiment where everyone hates everyone, and no one eats their lunch. Seriously, why didn't we ever eat our lunches? You knew where you fit in the social hierarchy based on the brand label on your jeans. The pecking order went from athletes to band nerds, with a lot of skateboarders and pot smokers in between.

At fourteen, I was terrified to be seen and equally scared to go unnoticed.

94

I was madly in love with a boy in my class. He was kind enough to tell me about all the girls *he* was madly in love with; none of whom ever happened to be me. In high school, I spent most of my energy trying to look like everyone else. And while there were good times and fun moments, nothing about those four years helped prepare me for the isolation and independence of college. #Thanksfornothinghighschool.

When I think back to everyday moments of high school, I squirm at the thought of how casual sexual assault was. When a girl is sixteen years old, she doesn't even understand what sexual assault is. For example, if Jimmy sticks his hands down your pants at a football game without permission, is that assault?

Everyone had secrets: bad grades, parents divorcing, eating disorders, and pretending you weren't gay. It was as if you had an entire cafeteria of adolescents pretending they were normal when no one even knew what normal was. If you were lucky, you got a solid group of girlfriends. There was also a lot of peer pressure to drink this or smoke that or make any number of other horrible life choices.

I used to tell people that I loved high school. But now that I have this six-year-old angel entering first grade, I don't want her anywhere near it. I'm praying she turns out to be a prodigy and can just skip right past it. I don't want her to have to see her name in black marker when she visits the restroom. I don't want her to think that when a boy gropes you, you should just play dead instead of defending yourself and reporting the assault. I don't want my daughter to be mean to kids who are already hanging on by a thread themselves. I need her to know who she is, whether she makes the volleyball team or not. I'll purchase a clarinet for her, and she can run lines at band camp if it keeps her off that creepy guy's radar.

I am not sure how to raise a daughter who can survive high school. My parents were great—beacons of light and wisdom. I swallowed affirmations like rock candy, and I still barely made it out alive. I want my daughter to be smarter than I was (a low bar, let me tell you), so I am starting now.

When she starts first grade, I am going to remind her always to share her crayons. When she walks into that lunchroom, I am going to tell her to sit with someone who looks alone. And when she is ready for junior high, I'm going to ask her what she understands about sex. I can't let the school system or the social order be the loudest voice in teaching my daughter how she can survive high school.

Life is going to come at us fast, y'all. I'm not waiting ten years to prepare her for the anxiety fest she is about to enter. When these tiny angels go to first grade, we have less than a decade to prepare them for the social experiment called high school. And we need to know that we did our best. Here is what I know: We cannot leave it to our churches to teach our kids about Christ. We have to do that. We cannot hope that a teacher stops and prays with them. We have to do that. God is literally the only thing that kept me believing that there was an actual plan for my life. I believed that I was designed because my parents introduced me to the Designer. Our kids will not survive high school if we aren't praying *for* them and *with* them right now.

I want my daughter to be better than I was in high school.

Bible Verse for Reflection
"I am reminded of your sincere faith, a faith that dwelt first in your grandmother Lois and your mother Eunice and now, I am sure, dwells in you as well" (2 Timothy 1:5, ESV).

Questions
- Share with your partner one bad memory from high school.
- What do you think that experience can teach you about parenting?
- Today, spend time in deep prayer for the people you love. They need it.

I'm Resigning as the Token Christian

Christ literally walked in our shoes.
—Timothy Keller

I don't have many friends who are conservative or highly religious. In the majority of my relationships going back to high school, I always wore the "Christian" badge in my interactions. I was the one that people called when they needed someone to pray with them. I was the girl that my guy friends would pull aside at parties to whisper in my ear, "You shouldn't be here." I'm the prude, the token Christian, the conservative, naive, sweet friend who actually believes that angels are real. To this day, some of my closest friends lie about smoking weed or having casual sex, because they are afraid it will taint my perception of them. (Side note: I have your Instagram handle. *I got receipts, bro.*)

Most of my life I have been pegged as the perfect, delicate Christian friend, and in a lot of ways, I started to buy what they were selling me. But then I discovered Jesus for myself and realized I am nothing like Him.

I try really hard to follow Christ, but guys, I'm not that good at it. Sure, I'm all, "Treat others as you would like to be treated" and "Love your neighbor as yourself" when I am in the church pew, but the second that a seventeen-year-old MickeyD's worker leaves the fries out of my Happy Meal, I'm not happy (or nice) at all. I'm snapping pics when they aren't looking and drafting my own version of mean tweets. Where is Christ in that? The Bible gives us explicit instructions to take care of the poor among us, but how many of us are actually living that? We preach from the pulpit about helping the homeless, but most of us wouldn't let Larry from the corner store mow our lawns without a security system. #AmIRight?

I've seen Christians who were "courageous" enough to "solve" the poverty epidemic by Facebooking about a man with a "Will Work for Food" sign and warning their entire network to not be bamboozled by this lowly scammer. Honestly, whether he spends my five dollars on a Subway sandwich or to feed his unhealthy addictions is between him and God. He didn't ask me to verify his tax returns; he asked whether I could spare some change. I'm not worried if he is using me. Whether I choose to humanize or dehumanize another human being is between God and me.

God didn't tell us to give to people who deserve it. You don't have to police your handouts. What if God wasn't giving the command to serve because it helps people? What if the act of caring for others, regardless of whether or not they deserve it, actually helps *us*? What if loving your neighbor isn't about showing others how loving you are, but rather about making you aware of your own bias?

We think being Christlike is a piece of cake until no one saves us a slice of the cake: no one acknowledges what a great person we are, no one mentions our name at the Wednesday prayer meeting, and no one favorites our humblebrag. I want to be a real Christian. One who serves silently but loves loudly. I don't need to be your token Christian friend. I want to be your real friend; one that you don't have to crop the edges of your life with. I want people to tell me when they mess up. I want them to know that my love isn't conditional; that their sins won't change the value I see in their humanity. I want to love people as Christ loves me.

I've been a hypocrite. I've played up my religiosity and downplayed my struggles. My idea of sacrifice has been letting someone cut in line at Starbucks without me pulling their hair. I want to stop being satisfied with just being kind and actually start seeking opportunities where I can make sacrifices for other people, regardless of whether they deserve it.

PS: God loves you. And I assure you, you don't deserve it.

I'm resigning as the token Christian. I wasn't all that good at it anyway.

I need my life to say more about God and His compassion than it says about me and mine.

Bible Verse for Reflection
"Those who consider themselves religious and yet do not keep a tight rein on their tongues deceive themselves, and their religion is worthless" (James 1:26).

Questions
- How are you being a hypocrite?
- What does loving people look like for you personally?
- How can you make a difference right now where you are?
- Ask your spouse to hold your tongue accountable.

She Was Flirting With My Husband

A good husband makes a good wife.
—English proverb

I was eleven the first time I saw a girl flirt with my husband. Technically, he wasn't my husband yet, but he had passed me two notes, so I figured it was close enough. He was using the numbers on his calculator to make funny words. She laughed every time he came up with a new one. I didn't get the joke.

I was far from being the prettiest girl in the classroom. My diary pages were filled with his last name beside my first name, and I wasn't sure what twist of fate would ever make that legal. My mother told me to just be myself. It's funny because most of my life I tried to be funny or popular or pretty, but I have had to learn what it means to be myself. The other girls kept giggling, but I stopped trying to impress him. He noticed. The notes grew more frequent and so did my confidence. In the sixth grade, my husband taught me that I shouldn't have to work hard to make a guy see me. I just had to be comfortable in my own skin.

Time has passed, and many things have changed. Nearly twenty years have danced between then and now, yet one thing has been constant—girls keep flirting. In many ways, I don't blame them. I've watched him go to pay for our food at restaurants and the pretty girl handing him change giggles. She tilts her head and strands of hair fall in front of her face. He pretends not to notice, but I know he sees her.

One time at a salon, the girl doing his trim asked if she could shave her number into his hairline. I watched him squirm with anxiety and awkwardly point to me sitting in the lobby holding our tribe of children. There are days that I am able to step outside of it and laugh at these encounters. And then there are days that I demand he wear his "I Heart My Wife" T-shirt. I have watched as girls flirted with my husband, yet I can honestly say that there has never been a day in our relationship that I have worried he would cheat or leave. Women may see his sparkling blue eyes, but I have seen his soul.

I know him. I know that he orders coleslaw as his side. I know that at least once every three months he will say he is a vegetarian again. I've watched him stare into the faces of three children I *gave* him within moments of them entering the world. I know the pattern that his lips fall into when he is embarrassed to have someone compliment him. I know to ignore him when he is angry, because thirty minutes later he will come back with an apology. I know that he stops at gumball machines. I know that when he goes on walks by himself it is because he feels spiritually disconnected and is hoping God will find him if he can just remove the obstacles that obstruct his view of heaven.

Girls in his past may have called him shy, but I know what has made him timid. I know how to make him feel confident, and I know which direction his tears will fall as he begs you not to leave. Girls who are smarter or prettier or wittier than me may notice him from time to time and smile in his direction, but I have never lost sleep over that. I know something that they don't: him.

I hear people talk about how they are looking for love or peace or fulfillment. They start jobs only to quit them because those jobs aren't the careers of their dreams. I know people who go from bed to bed, looking for the romance you see in movies. (It isn't real, by the way.) I've listened to friends talk about how they can't feel God anymore, so they quit talking to Him. They search for these things as if they might catch them if they just keep running. They won't.

In this world, you don't find love, you make it; you don't find peace, you earn it; you don't find fulfillment, you create it. These are not things you find; they are things you have to build. Love was never something that just happened to my husband and me; it's something we construct together. It's a journey. It's the culmination of experiences, shortcomings, and bright spots we have navigated together. It's the feeling we have as we look back over the past eight years and think about how we've climbed this giant mountain hand in hand. No one stumbles upon happiness. One has to make a decision to pursue it. It's not texts that pop up instantly or a lottery draw; it's handwritten letters that take years to craft. Purpose is always a journey.

My husband looks at life this way—as a voyage that you patiently fight through. He believes that sweat and hard work are the only paths toward fulfillment. And so when women flirt with him, I don't worry. There is only one road that leads him home.

As time keeps passing, I will only grow older; and if youth is beauty, it will escape me. With each wrinkle I earn, I have peace. I married a man who doesn't see lines but history.

So while girls may flirt with my husband from time to time, he'll keep pretending not to see them. No momentary thrill could ever replace the gratification he gets from standing at the top of this mountain we've climbed together.

I know something that girl doesn't: him.

Bible Verse for Reflection

"Place me like a seal over your heart, like a seal on your arm; for love is as strong as death. . . . Many waters cannot quench love; rivers cannot sweep it away" (Song of Solomon 8:6, 7).

Questions

- Have you ever seen someone flirting with your husband?
- Do you feel like your husband is trustworthy with other women? If not, explain to him how you feel.
- Is there anything you are struggling to forgive your husband for that involves another woman?

Relationships Aren't Vampires

*The only thing a person can ever really
do is keep moving forward. . . .
Take that big leap forward without hesitation,
without once looking back.
Simply forget the past and forge toward the future.*
—Alyson Noël

When I was in high school, I had a major crush on this guy I will call "Stuart." He started on the football team, played varsity all four years on the basketball team, and there were whispers of a college track for baseball. We met in the eighth grade. I had attended private school all my life; but in the middle of my eighth-grade year, I found myself seated in my town's public school for reasons that would require a whole other discussion. Stuart was the first boy, or person at all, to acknowledge my existence.

"You're new," he said, tapping my shoulder from behind in English class.

"I am," I responded sheepishly. I had talked to boys before, but not ones that didn't know what goes on a haystack. (It's an Adventist joke. Take my word for it.) I felt like a complete outsider. I had always been extremely well known in my small Seventh-day Adventist elementary school. For the first time in my entire educational existence, I knew what it felt like to be a stranger.

"I'll show you around," he said, smiling. And he did.

For the next five years, Stuart walked me to new classrooms, helped me to navigate a broken heart, invited me to his family dinners, made me cookie milkshakes, and told me how beautiful I was. I was fifteen. The only male who had ever told me I was beautiful was my father, and he liked me with ashy knees and no makeup, so I could hardly trust his judgment. When Stuart told me I was beautiful, I found myself hoping he was right. We shared a locker every year. He made me cards out of construction paper on Valentine's Day. He told everyone who would listen that I was his best friend, and each time he said it, I swallowed the lump in my throat that grew ever larger.

Eventually, I grew up. I went away to college. I was halfway through my freshman year when Stuart called me. He wanted to meet for dinner. We ate and laughed. He told jokes I pretended I had never heard before. He put his arm around me, and I felt the rejection fade. Nonetheless, he was too late.

That was the last conversation I ever had with Stuart. For the first time in our entire relationship, I wasn't the one being rejected. I guess since we didn't share a locker anymore, there was no need to keep pretending we were something that we weren't.

I teach communication courses. I have been studying communications for more than a decade and successfully defended my doctoral dissertation in June 2018. One of my favorite topics to walk students through is relationships. There are several communication theories dealing with how we start, maintain, and end relationships. Today I only want to walk you through one key concept, but I think it may be eye opening: it's the relationship cycle.

Relationships have six stages. The first stage is contact. In this stage, you meet. Some research suggests that within the first four minutes of meeting someone, you have already made up your mind as to whether or not you like that person.* In the four-plus years that I have been teaching, I have learned one thing about the theory of four minutes: typically, men stick with that first judgment.

---

* See Leonard Zunin, *Contact: The First Four Minutes* (New York: Ballantine Books, 1986).

This is important to note, ladies. It shouldn't take four years of locker sharing. Generally, four minutes does the trick. Funny side story: I was watching *Teen Mom* with my husband once. The girl asked the guy she was seeing, "What are we?" My husband immediately groaned.

"What's that about?" I asked him.

"I used to hate when girls would ask me that question," he said.

"What are we?" I was confused.

"Yes," he continued.

And then he said something I, to this day, wish a dude had told me at thirteen: "Heather, trust me, any time you have to ask a guy what you are, it's because you aren't. When a man wants to get married, he will make sure you know. If he wants to date you, move in with you, or is interested in you, he will make sure you know it. If he isn't saying it, it's because he isn't there."

I was stunned. I have told my students about this conversation each semester, and every time I see the same response from men—head nods. I had no clue.

The next stage of relationship development is involvement. This is when you test to see if your initial judgments were correct. You hang out in groups, you text, and you stalk social media accounts; you know, standard protocol.

The third stage of relationship development is intimacy. Here is something important about intimacy. It includes both private *and* social bonding. The couple has a private conversation about their relationship status and then makes the private commitment public knowledge. They tell friends, invite each other to meet their families, post it on Facebook, and so on.

I always tell my students that if you think you are in a relationship with someone because you are committing to each other privately, but that person does not ever make it public, you are not actually in a relationship. Affairs, casual sex, and secret texts are *not* real relationships. True intimacy is both private and public. If you are not experiencing both sides of intimacy, you simply aren't experiencing intimacy. Sorry if this is tough to swallow. I don't make the rules; I just teach them.

The fourth stage of relationships is deterioration. This is where relationship bonds weaken. Almost every relationship will go through deterioration, even healthy marriages. Some signs of deterioration are that the two of you talk less, show affection less, and hang out less. Don't panic! Deterioration is normal.

The fifth stage is repair. Nearly all relationships will go through forms of repair that should bring you back to intimacy. Remember, relationships are not broken just because they do not always stay in the third stage. This is normal relationship movement. The longer the relationship, the more you will find yourself bouncing from deterioration to repair and back to intimacy. It's normal. This doesn't mean you aren't meant to be together; it means you have a relationship.

The sixth stage of a relationship—the last stage—is dissolution. If the repair doesn't work, you end up here. Some people skip the fifth stage and head straight for dissolution. Dissolution says that your bonds are broken, and you separate both privately and publicly. It is a reversal of intimacy.

Here is what I think is bizarre: social media has completely changed relationship development. Stuart and I went through the six stages, and at the sixth stage, we stopped speaking. He recently (ten years later) sent a friend request on Facebook, but I still couldn't tell you what he is up to or what he does for a living. Frankly, I don't care. With the introduction of social media, however, many of us never enter stage six. We never truly end the relationship because, with the tap of a finger, we can see pictures, read thoughts, and relive old feelings.

This is totally rewiring the process. It's natural and normal for past relationships to die. Today we are perpetuating relationships forever. How does this affect our new relationships? How are our marriages affected by past relationships that never really die because of social media? How is stage three (intimacy) in our current relationship changed by the fact that we never fully went through stage six (dissolution) in our previous relationships?

If we keep a social book filled with old flames, we are fooling ourselves if we think it's impossible for one of those to spark and start a new fire. Do you want to know the biggest reason why we end relationships? Because there are potential alternatives available. Basically, the more options we have, the less likely we are to fight for our current relationship. If you or your partner are still friends with all your exes on social media, it tells your brain that you have alternatives available to you and decreases your dependence on your partner. When your relationship goes to the deterioration stage, which again is *normal*, you become less likely to fight for repair, which would have taken you back to intimacy. Why? Because of Stuart.

Social media can be credited with changing the way relationships are born, but it is also bringing along an interesting side effect: relationships aren't dying. This last point to me is as noteworthy as the first.

I did not write this to give you all the answers; I just wanted to raise some pertinent questions. Here is what I know: when I was eighteen and decided I was not going to be in a relationship with Stuart, we never spoke again, because why should we? Nearly 45 percent of first marriages end in divorce. By the way, more than one-third of divorce filings contained the word *Facebook.** Social media is a divorce lawyer's best friend.

We have to stop thinking that relationships should be eternal and that good things don't come to an end. It's simple communication theory. Every romantic relationship, except your current marriage, should experience stage six. There is a reason why couples stop sharing a locker when they break up in high school. Relationships were not meant to be vampires. Death is natural.

Bible Verse for Reflection
"Above all else, guard your heart, for everything you do flows from it" (Proverbs 4:23).

---

* Samantha Yule, "Facebook Now Crops Up in a Third of Divorce Cases Over Cheating and Old Flames," *Mirror*, January 20, 2015, https://www.mirror.co.uk/news/technology-science/technology/facebook-now-crops-up-third-5011205.

Questions

- Is there anyone on your social-media network that you need to delete?
- How do you think past relationships are affecting your marriage?
- Is there someone you wish your spouse would stop talking to?

The Memory Maker

The most beautiful things are not associated with money;
they are memories and moments. If you don't
celebrate those, they can pass you by.
—Alek Wek

I was nine years old. This would make my sister twelve. There is only a three-year difference separating us, but a lot of jealousy is buried between those three years. She got to do everything first. She hit puberty first, drove a car first, and had a boyfriend first, which led to a kiss that would also come first. When I was nine, my parents signed my sister up for horseback-riding lessons.

My family wasn't rich. My father always worked in ministry. He would tell me regularly, "The pay is not great, but my boss makes it worth it." It's funny because at the time, I knew we weren't rich, but I certainly never felt like we were poor. Looking back, that is all due to the efforts of my parents. My mom would forego a new suit for work if it meant that my sister could take horseback-riding lessons.

This left me jealous. Sure, I had gymnastics classes, swimming lessons, and a yearly summer camp ticket, but yet again Natasha was getting something I had never even thought to ask for. The lessons were an hour long, and so my mom used that time to get groceries, which left me as her companion. The sting of my sister galloping on horses while I was forced to push a shopping cart was short lived. I grew to love the trips with my mother. One time she got me a giant cookie slathered in frosting, and I can still see her head tossed back as she laughed at the mess I made eating it. Another time we pretended that my nachos were stowaways and made them walk the plank into my mouth. Some days we would run to the beach and watch the waves crash. Before I knew it, I genuinely waited for the day of horseback-riding lessons, because that meant alone time with my memory maker.

When I was in college, I remember daydreaming about what kind of mom I would be. I scribbled the words *memory maker* on my notepaper. I wanted to be the kind of mom that took a sharp right and hit the open road just before we turned into the school's parking lot. When my kids giggled, asking where we were going, I would not answer them. I would make them guess and become consumed in the anticipation of unexpected road trips. I wanted to have beach picnics like my mother gave me and be able to turn a mundane trip to the grocery store into an opportunity to create memories that they would hold on to, even twenty years later. I wanted to be a memory maker.

I failed. I have always had this insatiable drive to be successful. For the four years of my PhD coursework, I truly struggled to find a balance between my dreams for myself and my career and my duty as a mother and wife. Confession of a Christian wife, number 10,918: *We fail!* To be frank, my fantasies of becoming a memory maker were overrun by my need to prove myself professionally.

Then I started reading mom blogs. I looked at my friend Lauren. She talked about turning everyday routine into adventures for her three littles. I sifted through her newsfeed with photos of children with dirty feet and large smiles. She was doing it. She had created the fantasy world I had been failing at. I felt distinctly uncomfortable.

I made a pact before God this week to resurrect the memory maker. If I let what I do with my students or my research or my books overshadow what I am doing in my home with my children, I am failing not only them but also myself. Yes, I want to be successful; but if what I am doing on a stage is not superseded by what I am doing in the quiet of my home, then God is not pleased with me. I'm not successful; I'm self-focused.

The truth is that we can be replaced at work. We can be replaced in our ministries. We *cannot* be replaced in our marriages or with our children.

I wanted to write this for the other working mommas like me. Yes, your career is important; yes, it is part of what makes you, *you*; yes, you should pursue those things because it sets a beautiful example for your children about what hard work looks like. That said, don't stop pursuing them along the way. Our families are literally the greatest stamp we will leave on this earth. Motherhood and marriage can't be afterthoughts; they have to be our primary ministries. My mother is a successful, accomplished woman. But she was always my mother first. I never saw her leave my house without a kiss from my dad.

At my funeral, I don't want my children to have to list off the things I did for everyone else. I don't want them to list my books or achievements. I want them to talk about nachos. I want them to tell stories about pillow fights and road trips. I want them to have to sift into the piggy bank of stories we have collected and not be sure which one of the many to choose. I want to give them a rich life marked by the handprints of a memory maker.

When I was nine years old, my mother didn't give me horseback-riding lessons like I wanted. She gave me memories that I needed. Likewise, God may not give you want you want, but He always gives us what we need.

Bible Verse for Reflection

"Children are a gift from the Lord; they are a reward from him. Children born to a young man are like arrows in a warrior's hands. How joyful is the man whose quiver is full of them! He will not be put to shame when he confronts his accusers at the city gates" (Psalm 127:3–5, NLT).

Questions
- What memories do you have from childhood that really matter to you?
- How can you be intentional this month about making memories with your family?
- Break the routine today. Do something spontaneous with your family.

I've Forgotten Every Boy but One

Let the wife make the husband glad to come home,
and let him make her sorry to see him leave.
—Martin Luther

I have told my husband that the past is past. I say that I don't remember summer nights or the smell of sand. I've sworn that all memories of my life before have faded like cheap perfume. I play dumb, as if I have forgotten the touch of shaky hands. I'm lying. I've been close to forgetting this boy, but I can't. There are certain boys you never forget. Doesn't every girl have one?

Sometimes when I fight with my husband and I take time to clear my head, the boy I once loved haunts me. In moments when I least expect it, a flood of history surrounds me, and I'm watching the sunset off the pier. Maybe you aren't supposed to forget blankets draped with moonlight and days you laugh so hard you cry.

Days and weeks may pass, months even, and I won't think of him at all. But the second I let my guard down, I see a boy by a truck, motioning for me to come closer, and suddenly I'm twenty-two years old. There are no burdens, no keeping score, and no fights we have to work through. It's tattoos and long drives, riding on sheer adrenaline.

I'm a woman now. Those dusty flip-flops are long gone, but there is a tiny piece of me that treasures the time I spent with him. And I guess that's why I have let go of almost everything, except the memories.

There was a boy that looked at me in ways that I don't think husbands can, and it's not any fault of their own. When husbands see us, they see everything. They see kids and a mortgage; they see student loans and hospital bills. They see "I told you so's" and "Sorry, not sorry's." *Wives know where the bodies are buried, and husbands see that when they look at us.* All boys can see are tan lines.

Did you know that when I kiss my husband, there are nearly ten years of history pressed between our lips? We have laundry to fold and groceries to put away. We have errands to run and meetings to attend. There isn't much time for moonlight and blankets. Adrenaline is for teenagers. We haven't bought cologne since we were kids. We smell like coffee.

I am proud of the life we have built together, so sometimes I feel guilty when this one boy, on a starry night, creeps back into my mind. I find myself flooded in memories. Is that betrayal?

I knew a boy once that I can't forget, and he looked at me like I was a mystery. Every time he came near, I worried that he'd leave. There is something intoxicating about having someone but not fully having them. He was the flame and I was the moth. I overthought our conversations and rehearsed my words. He was new to me, and I loved studying him. There were so many nights that I didn't sleep till dawn because he was a book I couldn't put down. He was quicksand. Girls don't just forget boys like that.

At this point in my life, my husband can't make me feel the way the boy did then, and so I guess that's why I've never fully let him go. Sometimes I worry, because husbands know wives so well that one day I'll see tan lines and the sand will sting my face, and he will know.

I don't feel torn. You should know that. If I had to choose, I would pick my husband every time. Husbands are steady, they are committed, and they are everything a woman would need in order to feel safe and secure. That is why we marry them. Boys are none of those things. They can't be. *Time is a teacher, and there's not enough of it in quicksand.*

If I'm being honest, there is still a young girl in me who fantasizes about tattoos and freedom. I would love one shot of adrenaline.

I wonder if our husbands ever think of the girls who made them feel like they could do anything before we smothered them in logic and prac-ticality, before we told them they were fathers, and before we reminded them to buy milk. I wonder if they secretly think of the girls who rode shotgun on dirt roads that led to nowhere. I bet they do. There are some girls you don't forget, and I don't blame them.

That said, I'm proud of the man I chose. I still catch a glimpse of his wedding band in the sunlight and blush. On nights like tonight, with tiny bodies and small hands crammed between us in a king-size bed, I feel happy, at peace, and fulfilled. I wouldn't trade this.

So please don't tell my husband, but now and then when I fall asleep, I'll sneak off and see *the boy he used to be*. The boy who looked at me as if I was a mystery. I didn't know then who that boy would become. I couldn't have guessed that shaky hands grow steady. That he would trade moonlight-draped blankets for tiny cover hogs. He left parties for mid-night whimpers. He gave up adrenaline for routine and uncertainty for commitment. Summer days leave traces of a shaded line the girl in me likes to see—a small circle on his left hand, third finger. Tan lines can be tattoos. He is the rock of my life now. He reads his Bible with adoration and prays to God like they are friends. There is zero mystery. Every time we kiss, there is nearly ten years of life together pressed between our lips.

But tonight, while the whole house sleeps, I'll climb back into that truck. I'll reread pages I know by heart. I'll envision what it felt like to hope he'd still be here when the sun came up. I'll watch us laugh until we cry, and I'll sink into his quicksand. I love who we are, but I like to remember who we were.

Please, don't tell my husband this, but I've forgotten every boy but one. Because there are some boys that girls just don't forget.

Bible Verse for Reflection
"Kiss me and kiss me again, for your love is sweeter than wine" (Song of Solomon 1:2, NLT).

Questions

- Talk with your partner about how things have changed from your dating days to now.
- Is there anything in your old life with your partner that you miss?
- Look for an old card, letter, or note that your spouse gave you. Read it together.

Sex Is Awesome

Women need a reason to have sex, men just need a place.
—Lowell Ganz and Marc "Babaloo" Mandel

I tend to be the friend my friends call when there is a relationship problem. I am certainly unqualified to be a therapist, but I have studied gender and communication for several years. I know enough to be dangerous. Any of my friends will tell you, if you call me because you are having a hard time with your husband and you are certain you don't love each other anymore, my response will always be the same: When is the last time you slept with him?

Of course, at this they snarl. "Sleep with him? I can't sleep with him." Then they go on to list a slew of reasons why they couldn't possibly have sex with the man they married. Once they finish, nearly teary eyed, I say the words they hope I won't: "Call me back after you start regularly sleeping with your husband." And you want to know a secret? They rarely have to call me back.

Sex is important. Of course, sex alone isn't enough, but it also cannot be overlooked—that goes for men *and* women. Whether you want to or not, your relationship needs it. Trust me, I get it, watching *Survivor* in your underwear while sharing a sleeve of Double Stuf Oreos is just as romantic a night to me as any. I have heard many women ask, "Does having sex actually matter when our relationship is based on such a deep level of friendship?" The short answer to that is yes. If it didn't matter, you wouldn't need a relationship. Your best friend can hold you while you cry and binge on Netflix with a cup of Noosa yogurt (a personal favorite). Your partner is supposed to be those things for you and more. Since I hate trying to convince people of anything by my sheer opinion, let me tell you why I say this.

For starters, sex is the only thing that you share with your partner that you do not share with anyone else. I am a communications professor, so trust me on this: sex requires a level of communication that you literally cannot experience otherwise. There is a certain level of trust and vulnerability that comes with the sexual experience that is bar none the most intimate emotional moment you can ever come across. Think about the things you say to your partner during sexual intimacy. It's the only time in your life you are *that* vulnerable with someone, and the communication you use reflects it. And let's also dispel one popular myth: studies have shown that while television and movies may depict marriage as the old ball and chain where sex goes to die, that just isn't supported by data.

On average, 61 percent of single people report not having sex in the last year. Twenty-five percent of married couples say they still have sex two to three times a week; only 5 percent of single people can say the same. Married people also report having better sex than single people.* When it comes to married sex life versus single sex life, it's no contest. Someone please alert the single boys.

So what do we do if our relationship is not in the 25 percent of couples who are having sex two or three times a week? It's actually a better fix than one might think: you just do it. Experts all agree that the best way to want more sex is to have more sex. Regular sex increases your desire for sex. The hormones you experience with your partner during sex will actually rewire your brain to want more, even if that desire was not initially there. If you wait till you are both "in the mood," you will probably watch a ship set sail—a sad ship that feels alone and rejected. No one wants to be on that ship.

---

* Natasha Burton, "Marriage Sex: The Truth About Sex After Marriage," *HuffPost*, April 18, 2012, https://www.huffingtonpost.com/2012/04/13/marriage-sex_n_1422644.html.

The problem with sex is that human beings are hardwired to want it, and if you can't have sex with your partner, you may be tempted to seek it elsewhere. The importance men place on sex is a stark one. Sex is extremely vital to how men show love. "Research consistently shows that between 80 and 90 percent of men view sex as the most important aspect of their marriage."[*] Your husband isn't being a pervert; it is literally part of how he shows you that he loves you.

Note that this is true for both men *and* women. It's a myth that women are always the ones holding out or lacking libido. Men can have a low sex drive, too, leaving their partners resentful and unfulfilled.

Marriage experts Gary and Barbara Rosberg found that the vast majority of married men indicate that female initiation of sex is among their top sexual needs.[†] He doesn't just want to be having sex with you—he wants to know that you want to be having sex with him. This is something women get wrong all the time. Men are actually pretty vulnerable, and they feel more masculine when the women they choose to spend their entire lives with still desire them. Remember that. It's not enough for you to just "let him" have sex with you, he needs you to initiate sex, to *want* him. For most men, sex cannot be separated from love. So when you reject his sexual advances, you are rejecting love from him. For the average woman, talking, laughing, and sharing emotional intimacy are the primary ways they feel loved. You can see how so many couples have a problem.

Here's one more piece of data I found interesting: even if your partner is not asking for sex, studies show that men who minimize the importance of sex in their relationships do so out of past hurt or rejection and are trying to prevent future pain.

Some of us may have found ourselves in a relationship with the 10 to

---

[*] Juli Slattery, "Understanding Your Husband's Sexual Needs," Focus on the Family, accessed September 20, 2018, https://www.focusonthefamily.com/marriage/sex-and-intimacy/understanding-your-husbands-sexual-needs/understanding-your-husbands-sexual-needs.

[†] Gary Rosberg and Barbara Rosberg with Ginger Kolbaba, *The 5 Sex Needs of Men and Women* (Carol Stream, IL: Tyndale House, 2006), 81.

20 percent of men who don't identify sex as a primary need. It's normal in relationships for one partner to be less interested in sex than the other partner. Do it anyway.

Sometimes people don't need sex to express love. But your partner likely does. So do it for your husband. Do it for your wife. Plus, the more you do it, the more you will want to do it. The benefits of sex include better sleep, better intimacy, less stress, and even a stronger immune system. Sex is awesome, and you have a partner with whom you can enjoy the intimacy and deep connection that sex brings. God commanded Adam and Eve to be fruitful and multiply. God knows your marriage needs sex.

So the next time you are eating those Oreos while watching your favorite episode of *Law & Order*, surprise him. Hit the pause button and let him feel desired by you. I bet it will be pretty awesome.

Bible Verse for Reflection
"My lover is mine, and I am his" (Song of Solomon 2:16, NLT).

Questions
- Do you think you are having enough sex in your marriage? Please discuss this with your partner.
- When is the last time you initiated sex?
- Initiate sex with your husband. That is your homework.

Here's Why Sex Alone Can't Be Enough

*They slipped briskly into an intimacy from
which they never recovered.*
—F. Scott Fitzgerald

I already told you that the first time my husband ever called me was
the exact same night my engagement ended, two months before my
wedding. I hadn't seen Seth or spoken to him in two years. He had no
clue I had been engaged. Our very first phone conversation consisted of
me sobbing and him saying he was sorry. He asked if I wanted to hang
out the next night, and I wanted to do anything that would allow me to
escape the reality that I had paid for a wedding venue I would never use.

The next night he drove an hour and a half to see me. We let our feet
dangle off the edge of a pier. My eyes were puffy, my heart was broken,
and yet I felt a strange sense of peace in the presence of this tan boy with
blue eyes. After hours of sitting there, I realized I was laughing. My face
actually ached, but somehow laughing felt good. We sat together until
two in the morning, and before we parted, he leaned in to kiss me. I
backed away. I had too many emotions to process them all, but I knew I
didn't want to be kissed. We didn't even hold hands. On my first date with
my husband, I didn't give him one *hint* of sexual attention, yet somehow
I had given him something even more intense and valuable—intimacy.
When I talked, he listened, and as he stared into my eyes, I felt like
he really saw me. There is something intensely vulnerable about letting
someone see you, the real you. Not the Instagram you with flawless filters

or the Twitter you that's the perfect blend of wit and charm. There I was, fully clothed but naked in front of him on this beach. He saw me—a broken girl looking for answers on the edge of a pier, and somehow in his eyes at 2:00 A.M., I found them.

Sex is totally awesome, and also totally necessary, but sex outside of intimacy won't do a thing for you. First things first: SEX IS NOT INTI-MACY. I say that in caps because I am actually yelling it. Yesterday we talked about why sex is so important, unless you skipped yesterday, in which case I'm superoffended. Please rewind.

Today I want to talk about something I think a lot of us may not real-ize: sex won't make you fall in love. This is something my female students get wrong all the time. They actually think that because they are sleeping with someone, they are in an intimate relationship with that person. In Alice Fryling's book *Seven Lies About Sex*, she puts it this way:

> But the truth is that physical union, genital sex, is an expression of intimacy, not a means to intimacy. True intimacy springs from verbal, emotional, spiritual and physical communion.
>
> True intimacy is not primarily a sexual encounter. Intimacy, in fact, has almost nothing to do with our sex organs. A prostitute may expose her body, but her relationships are hardly intimate.*

One of the best things I ever learned in the field of communications is this: intimacy is not sex; it is self-disclosure. Yet girls all over the world are taking off their pants in hopes that this will make men stay. They think if they just sleep with a man often enough, sultrily enough, or intensely enough, he will never be able to leave. It simply isn't true. If you want to make someone fall for you, sex has to come *after* intimacy, and intimacy is something millennials seem to really struggle with.

We all fear rejection, but millennials seem to have mastered the art of running from it completely. Gone are the days where someone thinks

---

* Alice Fryling, *Seven Lies About Sex* (Downers Grove, IL: Intervarsity Press, 1997), 5.

another someone is cute, and so the boy or girl calls the cute person's landline and asks him or her out. That took guts. Today all one must do is send a friend request, hit the Like button, or download an app. The problem is that while these things may keep us safe from instant rejection, they also hinder us from one of the greatest elements of the human experience—connection.

A colleague came to me with a fantastic article about the science of falling in love. Because academics need to understand everything, it is not enough just to say someone "feels" a certain way when someone else is around. They have to put a logical order to everything, even love. So twenty years ago, Dr. Arthur Aron decided to do a science experiment in his laboratory. He wanted to see if there was a magic formula for making people fall in love. He brought in two strangers and had them discuss answers to thirty-six questions.* At the end, Dr. Aron told the strangers to stare into each other's eyes for four minutes without speaking.

The two strangers did fall in love, and they invited the entire science department to their wedding. Dr. Aron's theory is essentially that love is an action, not a feeling, and that by engaging in intimacy with your partner, love happens. Love thrives in an arena where trust and intimacy can occur. So while we can't force ourselves to love certain people, there are things we can do to try and foster those emotions, and intimacy is the key.

In communications, we teach that love is a blended emotion. What that means is that there are eight primary emotions, and all the other emotions are blended. In order to create certain feelings, you have to experience two different emotions at the exact same time; and out of those two emotions, love is born. Love is a blended emotion composed of *trust* and *joy*.

Hear me now: this is going to change your life. This is where I will blow

---

* Arthur Aron, Edward Melinat, Elaine N. Aron, Robert Darrin Vallone, and Renee J. Bator, "The Experimental Generation of Interpersonal Closeness: A Procedure and Some Preliminary Findings," *Personality and Social Psychology Bulletin* 23, no. 4 (April 1, 1997): 363–377, https://doi.org/10.1177/0146167297234003.

your mind. Any time you tell me how much you love your partner who keeps cheating on you, beating you, or hurting you, I will tell you that words have power, so we have to use them correctly.

Rather than say how much you "love" your partner who does these terrible things to you, I need you to remember that it is not possible for you to love someone you do not trust. Let me say that again, not sure if you heard me: love can only happen when you simultaneously experience the emotions of *trust* and *joy*. Blend those together and only then do you have love. You *cannot* have one without the other; no matter how many times you keep telling yourself that that is what you feel.

Love is *always* a safe place. So rather than excuse your partner's sins by saying you love him or her, be more specific. Say "I have so much joy with him, he just cheats on me"; "I have so much joy with him, he just hits me"; or "I have so much joy with him, he just hurts me."

I love words; but the reason I love them is that when we use them correctly, our relationships come into focus. Once we stop using *love* to excuse bad behavior—since we cannot experience love without trust—and we use the word *joy*, we realize how foolish we sound. I hope that then we can see clearly enough to reevaluate the relationship. By the way, you can love God. God is someone you can fully *trust*, and someone you can fully find *joy* in. God is love.

On my first date with my husband, I wouldn't even let him kiss me, and yet the intensity of our night together far exceeded anything I had ever experienced. Please tell all the young people you know that sex won't make you fall in love; but according to science, letting someone truly see you "naked" while fully clothed will.

Bible Verse for Reflection

"So Jacob worked seven years to pay for Rachel. But his love for her was so strong that it seemed to him but a few days" (Genesis 29:20, NLT).

Questions

- How would you describe the intimacy in your marriage?

- When is the last time you lost yourself in conversation with your partner?